Web Authority

Get It, Keep It, Reap the Profits

By

James "Doc" Stone

©2015

This book is dedicated to my patient and loving wife Diane who has stuck by me through all my passions. All my love to you

Special thanks to a few special people. Debbie Nicholson, thank you for all your time editing this book and wonderful words of encouragement. David smith, thank you for taking the time to read through this whole book end to end and really did a great job. Eileen Harvey, thank you for adding some special words when and where they were needed. Janet and Don Legere, thank you for supporting and believing in me and working together with me over the years to help me get to where this book was possible. Mike Filsaime, thank you for the opportunity to work with you and train your clients for quite a few years. It is when I came up with all these theories and was able to test them and work with others to see this through. Mike, a very special thanks for allowing me to make use of some of the perks a fellow like you gets and sharing them with me when you could. I cannot forget the effort of a special person in my life and someone I really admire. My mother Nancy is already an author of a book called "iguanas on my roof" which chronicles our lives and my childhood overseas in a turbulent time in our history. Your expert editing and guidance was crucial to finally getting this finished and into a form I am proud of. It was so fun working with you on this project.

Contents

WEB AUTHORITY – INTRODUCTION

ADVANCED ARTICLE MARKETING – That is what you are thinking this book is all about. Yes, it is, and so much more. Article marketing is just one component of the art of providing content to the world to attract traffic to your website. We are talking about *free traffic to your website and* only "White Hat' marketing practices." Coupled with a strategy that incorporates article writing for your blog, article writing for article marketing websites, syndication, and some simple secrets to writing an effective traffic grabbing article, you can achieve that proverbial golden ring in the sky for Internet marketers called an *Authority Website* within a surprisingly short period of time.

Web Authority is the idea that, for your topic, and your niche, you own the majority of the free, organic search traffic available. *Your site becomes the recognized authority on that subject.* That means your site is recognized not just by loyal readers, but more importantly, by all the major search engines. By the time you finish reading this book, you will know exactly how, where, and what to do to achieve this valuable and effective goal.

Wait a minute, why does this matter? Who cares if you are the authority site? What is all of this going to do for you? These questions should be answered before you spend the next few hours reading this book.

The answers affect your pocketbook. If you or your company is selling products or services on the Internet, you clearly want as much Internet traffic from the search engines as possible. The more visitors, the more chances you have of making a sale. The game of "Sales" is a game of numbers. More visitors equal more sales. What are you spending for that traffic, both in time and money? The article marketing game does not cost anything more than the time it takes to write the articles and to play the game. If you currently have an active Google AdWords pay-per-click campaign going, you know how much paid advertising can cost. It can be staggering if you are not careful.

Achieving *Web Authority* for your niche brings you targeted organic *free* leads. These are the kind of leads that some companies pay upwards of $100 each. It is worth doing, but even more than that, becoming the recognized expert in your industry or niche also brings trust from your prospects. These kinds of relationships with potential clients may take you months to cultivate in a traditional sales methodology.

Why doesn't everybody do this? Frankly, people do not like to write. I start my online webinars with this sentence "Really Doc, do I have to write stuff?" Yes, you do. The Internet after all is a collection of words and phrases. I understand how hard it is to write. When I wrote this book, I had most of it dictated and transcribed from my live webinars. This is one way of capturing original material for publication but there are so many other ways to get the content you want for next to nothing. We will cover that.

For now, you can relax. If you hate to write, you will be pleasantly surprised to know you can get around most of it and still get great results. If you love to write, this will be fun for you. I do want to remind you though. The reason we're writing is to provide search engines what they crave. Remember, the entire Internet is made up of nothing but words and some HTML code. Search engines cannot see pictures, they cannot get the gist of what you are trying to say, and they don't comprehend ideas like humans. Search engines must index your pages in a split second but there are more websites than people on the planet. They do not have time.

Search engines are searching for patterns. These patterns of words are called keyword phrases. There is a fine line between creating an article built for the search engines and an article that still makes sense and captivates a human. I will show you how to do both easily and with quality. The main reason most of us write articles is to attract website traffic and make a good living, but what we would really like is *free* website traffic from search engines. So for you writers out there, this will be fun. For the rest of us, we will concentrate on making this routine and purposeful.

WHERE DO YOU START?

What is the best way to build a website storefront to attract clients and build traffic to your site to become a catalyst for your business? How can you build an authority website so the search engines will send you more clients than you can handle? How can you write the right kind of content that attracts the search engines and all those clients? Where do you start?

As you consider these questions, you have to decide how to put your website together. Already you realize you did not want to be a programmer and it is a lot harder than it looks. And even if you learn how to be at least a pretty good HTML page builder, what should be the actual structure of the website that will be your storefront?

People have been building websites for years. They usually hire a web designer or buy some software to help make their webpages. They post a webpage and maybe even a few other pages to add some content and they think, "Okay, now all I need to do is let the search engines do their thing and I will be rich". Wrong, it just does not work that way. In fact, because there are more websites than there are people on the planet, your website is virtually invisible to the world. In addition, unless you register with some of the major search engines, your site could be considered just a here today, gone tomorrow anomaly.

This book will show you what to do, how to structure your site, what to write, and how to create a website that will attract as much traffic as you can handle.

The Structure

Over the years I discovered the best structure of a website should be one that most anyone can do themselves or with a little help. It is come from consulting with thousands of people and seeing what they have done, noting the mistakes they made, and what created their success. My conclusion: only a very basic setup is needed. I call it an *Internet Sales Funnel.*

WHAT IS A SALES FUNNEL?

What is a sales funnel? Why do they work better than anything else? And why would this work in almost any kind of business? Yes, there are all kinds of variations. The bottom line is that this brand of sales funnel gives you a single place to advertise (maximizing your ad dollars spent), a single list, a single blog to administer, and a single squeeze page (A squeeze page is designed to help add people to your newsletter). It is easy to understand and build, and it is scalable. There is a place to put all of the products or services you have ever tried and products or services you will add. It will grow with you no matter how big you get. And it is yours. You are in control. You get all the profit. You pay affiliates, if you have them, but you are the boss. Now you can focus on your own business, your own future and you never have to look back. And your business choice can be just about any topic you can think of so you can enjoy it and understand it. The issue is what to sell and how to monetize your favorite subject to make a full time living from it. We will cover that later. Let's concentrate on a format first.

If you need help deciding what your topic for your business

should be, join our community at the link below. When you get

click the link in the opt-in email you receive, scroll down to the

bottom for three free gifts. One of those webinars is all about what

to sell and why and how to monetize it.

http://www.Internetsalesfunnel.com

You need one place to advertise. What so many people do is have twenty-five different unrelated products or services from twenty-five different sources and they like all of us have limited resources. They take their entire one hundred dollar budget and spread it around to each product. That is four dollars each. Four dollars is not enough

4

to pay for the first ad for the first product. Of course it does not work, nothing happens. So they decide they should choose one product, try and advertise it and see what happens. Maybe they get some signups, maybe they do not, so they try another, and then another. It is like trying to hit the side of a car with a pea shooter from one thousand yards. You will not be successful, you need one place to consolidate all your advertising dollars and work on defining and refining your offer so your conversions (conversions = clients that buy = sales) increase. In short, you need a funnel with a single refined entry point.

Once a potential client signs up to your newsletter, even if they do not buy something right away, over time they will discover everything you have to offer. Hopefully, at least one product will interest them enough to become a client.

You only need one list of prospects. You could have two lists as opposed to just one, perhaps "buyers" and "potential buyers", but to get started, you only need one. I've seen folks with upwards of one hundred different lists for every crazy purpose. They do not have a funnel, so they instead have a separate list for every product and project. Sometimes that is necessary, but not if you are concentrating on your own product or products. Having that many lists means you need separate webforms (HTML code that allows people to sign up to your newsletter) for each list, and separate email follow-ups for each list. It is just way too much work. Can you imagine trying to create email follow-ups of at least fifteen emails for one hundred different lists?

There are some out there that say you do not need a list at all. There is not one successful Internet marketer out there that will tell you that. With no list, you must constantly advertise, but with a list of 100,000, it costs nothing to send an email and almost any offer you make will net you at least a few sales. Some people do not buy right away. It can take an average of six or more emails to make a sale, especially with large ticket items. If you have no list, you will never find out. Do not be fooled into thinking that building a list isn't one of the most important things you will do.

You only need one email address. Some people have tried to have a separate email address for every website they own. That may sound like the proper business practice, but who has time to login and check forty-five email addresses every day. When you start getting busy, you will not have time. There has to be a better way. Fortunately, there is a better way. Please keep reading.

You need a blog. Not just any blog, but a WordPress blog. Blogs are infinitely better at attracting what is called organic traffic from the Internet to your site. This is free traffic. Paid traffic is one thing, but organic or free traffic is what happens when someone is doing a search on the Internet and they find you all on their own. You have optimized your site for whatever keyword phrase they just typed in and your site comes up in Google or Bing or some other search engine. "SEO" or Search Engine Optimization is a confusing subject and what works and what does not is constantly changing. One thing is clear. WordPress is a very unique tool to attract organic traffic. There is nothing else like it. Your WordPress blog sits in the root of your website. The blog will be about your topic.

Choose your topic carefully. Some people try to manage ten or fifteen blogs at once. Blogs require articles. It is hard enough trying to keep material added to your blog. Keeping ten or fifteen blogs current is an almost inhuman task and the reality is in this business if you aren't moving forward, you are falling behind.

WordPress Blogs have what they call RSS (Really Simple Syndication) news feeds. What it means is that new news gets listed with priority over old news. That is bad if you do not keep at least one article a week going. It is good because if you do, you will rapidly move ahead of all of those who do not keep up.

WordPress Blogs have the ability to be listed in more than one search engine. Did you realize that Google has three major search engines? The three search engines are the regular one you use every day, one that is called a blog search, and one that is called a News Search. WordPress Blogs come built-in with blog search capability but a piece of software called a plugin must be installed to get your pages listed in the regular search engine. Blogs have the ability to be listed in two of these three types of search engines. (The News Search engine is specialized to the publishing industry). That is unique; nothing else can make that claim.

WordPress Blogs allow every single post to be search engine optimized for the regular and blog search engines. If you write one article a week that is optimized for a researched keyword phrase and do simple SEO for each article, you would have fifty-two optimized pages optimized for both search engines in a single year. Most websites, even the major manufacturers, only SEO their main pages. The bottom line is that having a WordPress Blog as your organic traffic attractor sitting in the root of your site is a major advantage over every other kind of site.

What about squeeze pages? If you only have a single entry to your funnel and a single list, then you only need one squeeze page. A squeeze page is a page that has what is called a webform. It is a bit of HTML code put on a page on the Internet that a potential client could fill out with their name and email. They press a button and *opt-in* the first time. They receive an email with a link to *opt-in* a second time. By *double opting* into your newsletter, they agree to receive additional emails from you. They are now added to your newsletter. You may have several squeeze pages in the beginning of your marketing efforts as you try to refine your offer. You might do what we call split testing. Split testing allows each version of your squeeze page to be evaluated for its effectiveness. Once your page is converting like you want, you will only have one. A high converting page means that visitors to the page are completing the webform and are being added to your newsletter. You want the highest percentage of visitors to new members of your newsletter as you can. By people signing up to your newsletter, a squeeze page builds your list. People have to sign up to find out about your offer. You will drive any paid traffic to your squeeze page while your WordPress blog sits and gathers the organic traffic. In order to have a webform on your squeeze page and a list, you use what is called an *autoresponder*. The autoresponder gives you all the tools you need to build your list except the squeeze page itself. Using the autoresponder, you will pack it with follow-up emails that go out automatically and tell all your prospects (the people on your list) about everything else you have to offer. An autoresponder is called an autoresponder because it sends out automatic emails immediately and periodically after a prospective client adds themselves to the list. You write the emails once as many as you want and it all happens automatically.

It is scalable. By adding a few optimized pages to your WordPress blog and a few follow-up emails in your autoresponder for every product you have, have had, or will have, you can grow your product as big as you like.

And it is easy to understand and build. You can build your site from scratch without all the expense that most people end up spending. What you need is all the resources at your fingertips in a library where you can start and stop the step-by-step presentations until you catch up. You need some help. You need a community of people in the same boat you can draw from and help them as well.

If you would like to join our community and find out about live

webinars and have the kind of training and resources I'm

discussing in this book, get signed up for notifications at

http://www.Internetsalesfunnel.com

You must have 5 elements in your Sales Funnel

1. Products and/or Services to Sell

2. Domain of your own

3. WordPress Blog

4. Squeeze Page

5. Autoresponder

You need products and/or services to sell.

You need a website of your own. Not someone else's. This is going to be your product or products you choose, in a particular niche you choose. You can pay affiliates to help you, or you can keep all the profits. You will not be dependent on anyone else.

You need that WordPress blog sitting in the root of your site and some place to put your search engine optimized articles.

You need a squeeze page to drive traffic to and to build your list. At first, you may have several as you develop your offer and refine it until you get the kind of conversions you are looking for.

You need an autoresponder in order to build a squeeze page and send out automated emails.

Pretty simple, isn't it? It is easy to understand, but the details are where the rubber meets the road.

The structure of your site will look like this. The WordPress blog will be in the root of your website. You can put the squeeze page almost anywhere in the site, but it is usually placed with all its parts in a folder. All your product pages will be in your blog as posts or in folders as HTML pages. And your autoresponder will be using one of many available services already available and inexpensive. The resource area at the end of this book has a few great suggestions.

Here's a sample structure of what I'm talking about:

http://www.jamesstone.com – blog, squeeze

http://www.jamesstone.com/product1

http://www.jamesstone.com/product2

http://www.jamesstone.com/product3

http://www.jamesstone.com/product4

Add anything else you want.

WHY A SALES FUNNEL?

A sales funnel as I have defined it has a single blog. It is not going to overly stress you out trying to keep up. You will have to write articles for your blog. If you want to attract free traffic from the Internet, you have to write something, whether you borrow it, curate it (Make old content new), or make it up on your own. It does not matter where you get your material as long as it is original and related to your topic. If you borrow content or curate the content the end result should be as original as possible redone in your own words. I must emphasize that the Internet is made up of words and phrases as far as search engines are concerned. The search engines cannot see the pictures, just the words and patterns of words. Part of your business is providing the search engines what they crave. Give them what they want and they will give you what you want. They give you traffic.

Doc Stone Tip: If I repeat some idea here in this book, it means it is really an important concept to keep in mind as you try to understand what I'm describing. Some of the ideas in this book are very technical. They are being described in such a way that anyone should be able to grasp the concept. Hopefully I manage to accomplish my goal of making technical material easy to understand. I feel that repeating something I may have said earlier applies to what is being said now and must be emphasized or the idea falls apart. Many people will be reading this book from all walks of life and all levels of technical expertise. If I offend you in any way by repeating certain concepts, it is not my intention.

Here is one of those repetitions.

You need a single squeeze page and a single place to advertise to consolidate your advertising dollar. You need is a single list. Why complicate things. Focus on one thing. Focus on just you and your product. For that, a single list will do. It is easy to manage and understand what you are doing and what you are trying to accomplish. It is scalable. It will grow with you no matter how big you get and I want you to grow, so do you.

It will be a fair amount of work at first to get your first sales funnel built. Once it is built, your life will get a lot easier. You really can spend just a few hours a day tweaking your system and doing your marketing. And if it takes more time than that, it will mean you are packing and shipping and invoicing, managing your money, and paying affiliates. That is all good stuff, and that is why you make it about you and things you like and are interested in. If you are like a lot of us out here making a full time living on the Internet, you will find yourself working hard and spending a lot of time at this. Why? Because you will find out doing what you love is fun. It won't feel so much like work anymore. You can make this as little or as much work as you want it to be, but make it something you enjoy.

This book is about Article Marketing, isn't it? Yes, it is, but not the way it used to be taught. The old ways don't work anymore. It is about creating your own *Web Authority*. I covered the structure of what I call an Internet Sales Funnel because if your blog is sitting somewhere in a folder, then it is not doing its job and will not be effective. The blog MUST be in the root.

A sales funnel starts with a WordPress blog that sits in the root of your website using your name or your name and a word describing your business as the domain name. The blog sits there attracting organic traffic off the Internet from free searches on Google and Bing and the rest of the search engines. The blog has articles about every product you sell related in such a way that it all makes sense. You need a squeeze page where you drive all your paid traffic, paid traffic from Safelists, Traffic Exchanges, Ad Rotators, and pay-per-click sources.

You want to add people to your list (your newsletter). To build your list, you will require an autoresponder service. You will add follow-up emails to the autoresponder about everything you do. You need sales pages and/or affiliate pages for each product you sell.

Get the first three or four products or services done so you can start marketing your sales funnel and making an income. Then you add everything else later.

Typically, some of the traffic methods you will use to drive traffic to your site will be things like *Search Engine Optimization (SEO), Safelists, Traffic Exchanges, Ad Rotators, Social Networking, Autoresponders, Squeeze Pages, Blogs, Swaps, and Article Marketing.* Article marketing today is not the same as it was five years ago. It is not about publishing articles on article marketing directory websites so much anymore. It is about an all-inclusive article marketing strategy that includes publishing articles on article marketing sites and publishing certain types of articles on your blog. I have added a few tested SEO secrets here and there.

Blogs have things called tags. Tags are keyword phrases, tags get indexed in a search engine you probably have never heard of called Google's Blog Search. Regular Google Search requires what is called a plugin. A plugin is a piece of software that is added to a WordPress blog that gives the blog some new capability, much like an App is to a cellphone. I use the All-in-One SEO plugin but there are several that will work. This gets you indexed in Standard Google Search. What is unique to a blog is that each Page can command a different keyword phrase. Blogs are also News based. That means that newer articles are ranked higher than older articles on the same subject. Blogs also have what is called RSS (Really Simple Syndication) or News Feeds which are listed and can be listed in many other places on the Internet. Finally, most websites have a limited scope of the pages that can be built while blogs allow virtually unlimited content.

If I were to rank the different types of blogs, WordPress is definitely my top choice. How do you use WordPress to accomplish all I'm claiming? It is through my brand of Article Marketing.

THE DEFINITION

The Old Definition

Internet article marketing is used to promote the author's expertise in their market and about products or services online via article marketing directories. Article marketing directories with good web page rank receive a lot of site visitors and may be considered authority sites by search engines, leading to high traffic. These directories then give PageRank to the author's website and in addition, send traffic from readers. That is the definition from Wikipedia.

Business Owners, Marketers and Entrepreneurs attempt to maximize the results of an article advertising campaign by submitting their articles to a number of article marketing directories. However, most of the major search engines filter duplicate content to stop the identical content material from being returned multiple times in a search engine results page. In short, these articles should be unique, never before published articles.

That is pure Article Marketing the old way.

The New Definition

I define Article Marketing today as an all-around approach that includes pure article marketing on article marketing directory websites combined with traffic-attracting articles published on an author's website. There are a number of different article types to be written and each has its own purpose. Article marketing directories with good web page rank receive a lot of site visitors and may be considered authority sites by search engines leading to high traffic. These directories give page rank and act as a medium to create one way links to the author's site. An author's own articles published using search engine optimization techniques designed to attract organic traffic from both blog search and regular search engines add to the overall traffic. The links and traffic combine to create an authority site with very high page rank.

The primary goal behind article marketing is to get search engine traffic to the article so the author can strengthen their *authority* and influence within their field, while also leveraging that traffic for their own site(s). The key to article marketing is that *the author should be providing value with their articles,* not just promoting their site, products or services.

Most forms of search engine optimization and Internet marketing require a domain, Internet hosting plan, and promoting budget. However, article marketing makes use of article marketing directories as a free host and receives traffic by way of organic searches due to the listing's search engine authority. We're going to combine the two and make the best of both worlds. So there is your definition. It sounds wonderful but how do you do that?

BUILDING TRAFFIC

The Idea is, each week or more often, choose a product or topic. Use a keyword tool like Google Keyword Tool now in AdWords or tools like Webfire to research keyword phrases related to what you want to write about. I will detail where and how to use these tools later.

> If you would like to join our community and find out about live
>
> webinars and have the kind of training and resources I'm
>
> discussing in this book, get signed up for notifications at
>
> http://www.Internetsalesfunnel.com

Then you research the keyword phrase using Google searches to look for competitors. Once you have determined the keyword phrase you will use, write the post. Track it using analytics and watch your traffic and sales grow. Analytics is the study of traffic visiting your site using software readily available and easy to use. By studying the results, you can improve the effectiveness of your marketing tactics.

The big secret here is how you write the article.

THE SECRET

The big secret is to find the keyword phrase that has little competition and great traffic *first*, and then write the article. What everybody does is write a great article and then try to figure out what keyword phrase works best after the fact. That sounds too easy, doesn't it? That is because there is much more to it than just these two short sentences.

If you are good at writing articles already, this will be easy. What if you are absolutely terrible at writing anything? First, that is a cop-out. Remember I said the Internet is *all* words, phrases and patterns of words. It stands to reason that writing articles, publishing, creating pages of some kind is always going to be a big part of your job. I suggest you resolve to get better at it. There is lots of help. You do not have to dream up much of anything on your own or even write them yourself if you know where to look.

So here is the mechanics of writing an article in your blog that is designed to attract and pick up organic free traffic from the Internet.

This is typical structure of a WordPress Post.

Title

Body

WordPress Tags

Page SEO (Title, Description, and Keywords)

It all starts by finding a keyword phrase related to the topic you want to write about. For this step, you need a keyword tool. Google used to provide a free tool that worked pretty well. Now you have to have a Google AdWords account to use their tool and it is a little harder to figure out. I use a tool called Webfire but it does cost money. (Webfire is priced from $41/mo. to $99/mo.) I find a tool like Webfire saves me money, but there are other tools out there such as Keyword Spy, SemRush, and Keyword Eye. Any of these will do the job.

What you are looking for is a keyword phrase, usually from four to seven words long. It depends on how unique the words are. The more unique, the fewer words you will need, but never less than three. The tags in WordPress can be less words but the standard Google Search Engine will usually be four or more. Remember, tags are keyword phrases for Google's blog search engine. You will choose one main keyword phrase and from twelve to fifteen more related phrases. We will discuss why later.

Once you have chosen your keyword phrase, do a little research. Go to Google, type the phrase in and see the results. A lot of keyword tools only return USA search engine results. You may not be in the USA, and you may be marketing to the whole world, not just one country. You can review what your competition is using for keyword phrases by right-clicking on their sites, select "view source" and look for the keywords Meta tag. In addition to the Meta tags, also look in the body of the page and see how many times your phrase is being used. You want to have an idea just how many times you will need to use your keyword phrase in the article you are going to write. The idea is to use the phrase one more time than your competitor. Meta tags are short instructions written in HTML code meant for search engines. The main ones are the Title, Description, and Keywords (TDK). Meta means information about information, much like the index cards are information about the information in books in a library.

```
<!DOCTYPE html PUBLIC "-//W3C//DTD XHTML 1.0 Transitional//EN" "http://www.w3.org/TR/xhtml1/DTD/xhtml1-transitional.dtd">
    <html xmlns="http://www.w3.org/1999/xhtml"
        xmlns:og="http://opengraphprotocol.org/schema/"
        xmlns:fb="http://www.facebook.com/2008/fbml"
        xml:lang="en" lang="en">
    <head>
    <link href="/web/fitness/fitness.ico" rel="shortcut icon" />

    <title>Weight-Loss Plans</title>
    <meta http-equiv="Content-Type" content="text/html;charset=UTF-8" />
    <meta name="description" content="Weight-loss plans for everyone, including daily weight-loss plans, weekly plans, and strategie
<meta property="fb:admins" content="1561780258" />
<meta property="fb:app_id" content="674728008277" />
    <meta property="fb:page_id" content="134195577441" />
    <meta property="taboolatrack" content="false" />
<link rel="canonical" href="http://www.fitnessmagazine.com/weight-loss/plans/" />
                    <script type="text/javascript"
                    src="/web/js-min/js/mdp/util/modern.sr.js"></script>
    <script type="text/javascript" src="/web/js/mdp/lib/jquery/jquery.js"></script>
    <script type="text/javascript" src="/web/common/js/lib/swfobject/swfobject.js"></script>

    <script type="text/javascript">
    /* <![CDATA[ */

    /* MDP namespace */
```

Right Click on Any Page to Display Meta Tags

Choosing the phrase itself is probably the hardest part of all this. If you hate writing, you want this article you will be laboring over to count and to pull in as much free traffic as it can. If you are like most of us, you do not just sit down to write an article for fun. Choose your phrase well and make it count.

Now you are ready to write your article. Use the Keyword Phrase in the title. Use the keyword phrase at least twice in the body of the article. If you can, bold one of them, and even better, make the other one a link to another page on your site. Finish your article with at least

250 words, but be aware that 400 is the minimum for some articvle marketing directory sites. How many words is enough? Enough words are really what make sense to the person who will someday be reading it. If you have a lot to say, break it up into two articles and find another keyword phrase to use for part two. Now, do your tags. Use the phrase as one of the twelve to fifteen tags. The other tags are the other eleven to fourteen phrases you found earlier. Tags get you listed in Google's Blog Search Engine.

Tags

| | Add |

Separate tags with commas

weight loss plan   weight loss diet   best weight loss diet   diets for weight loss   rapid weight loss diets   healthy weight loss diet

Choose from the most used tags

WordPress Tags Area Example

Finally, use the phrase in the All-In-One SEO Plugin area. There will be a title, description, and keywords area. You guessed it. Use the phrase in the title and the description and one of the twelve to fifteen keywords.

All in One SEO Pack

Upgrade to All in One SEO Pack Pro version

Title: Weight Loss Plan

16   characters. Most search engines use a maximum of 60 chars for the title.

Description: My Weight Loss Plan has worked for me. Read about my experiences here.

71   characters. Most search engines use a maximum of 160 chars for the description.

Keywords (comma separated): or weight loss, rapid weight loss diets, healthy weight loss diet

Disable on this page/post:

The first article is done, but there is one more part to my secret. **Doc Stone Tip:** Make the first article part of a twelve to fifteen article *power block*. Write an article for each of the twelve to fifteen keyword phrases you found using each one in the same manner. Each article should be unique, not spun, using the ideas for the article in a different manner. You will not be spinning the same article twelve to fifteen times. You are writing unique articles based on the keyword phrases you found.

Spinning

Some marketers attempt to circumvent writing unique, never before published articles by creating a number of variations of an article, known as article *spinning.* By spinning an article and publishing many versions of the same article, one can theoretically acquire site visitors from a number of article marketing directories. That is just not necessary and it is the wrong way of going about it. In short, do not buy spinner software. It is a waste of money. Not only that, Google is cracking down so hard on duplication, you will hurt your efforts. *Don't do it!*

What you have done now is create a block of articles designed specifically to pull in traffic for a particular keyword phrase group that, after doing some research was under-served in Google's Search Engine. You have done the SEO work just a little bit better than your competition. You want to do just one phrase better than your competition, no more.

Does this work? If you have done enough up front research on the keyword phrase, yes it works every single time. Will you hit the jackpot every time? Of course you won't. Some articles will be better at attracting free traffic than others. A lot depends on the uniqueness of the words, but mostly it will depend on the competition for that keyword phrase and the level of SEO competence of your competition. You should be writing at least one article a week as part of your job at home. In fact, with the Google Blog Search engine, they will forget you exist after one week. If you do what I'm suggesting and each article brings in a meager 500 hits a month and you do this for one year, you are looking at twenty-six thousand *free* hits a month.

What is interesting about this is that the twenty-six thousand may be a low estimate. A site that has that much traffic, that many links, and original articles as an authority site gets ranked higher by the search engines so they throw even more traffic at you. This is *free* traffic and it is *targeted* traffic. The kind of people coming to your site did a search on the Internet, used the keyword phrase you used, found you, and realized that yes that *is* what they looking for. That kind of traffic makes sales. This distinction between targeted traffic and just any old traffic is important. If you are getting traffic from a safelist or a traffic exchange (safelists and traffic exchanges are paid methods of obtaining traffic to your site, usually only frequented by other Internet marketers) for example, those people aren't looking for a solution to whatever problem that your product solves. Other Internet marketers frequent safelists and traffic exchanges in the hopes of increasing their own traffic. Traffic considered organic is people searching for you are looking for a solution to a problem. Organic traffic means someone has a problem, they enter some words into a search engine and some possible sites are returned. They choose one and visit that site. They are looking for a solution to a problem and will buy the solution from you if you have a fair price and it is exactly what they need.

SAFELISTS AND TRAFFIC EXCHANGES

Safelists and traffic exchanges are considered by some to be black hat traffic generation tools. I do not agree. A safelist allows you to send emails to the list of people who are members of that safelist unsolicited. In order to become a member of a safelist, you must agree to receive emails from other members. Traffic exchanges allow you to receive visitors from other members of that traffic exchange and in return you agree to surf the other member's websites for a certain period of time. People who use safelists and traffic exchanges have agreed at least twice to surf your sites and receive emails from you. Therefore it's not spam. People who surf traffic exchanges and receive emails from safelists are people like you and me and if you have a product that appeals to other Internet marketers, they can both be very useful.

CONTENT IS KING

REALLY, I HAVE TO BE A WRITER?

If you want to attract free traffic from the Internet, you have to provide words and phrases to the search engines. You have to write something, whether you borrow it, curate it, or make it up on your own, it does not matter where you get your material as long as it is original, and on topic. Again, when I say borrow or curate, it does not mean to copy and paste it. It means rewrite it using your own words. Part of your business is providing the search engines what they crave. Give them what they want and they will give you what you want. They give you traffic and they give you links. The more traffic you have and the more times the search engines find you by following links from other websites, the more traffic they send you. The traffic grows heavier the longer you keep at it.

We have been discussing how to build your site, how to put it together, what its structure should be, what kind of products it is going to have - the works. We are now down to traffic. This is exciting stuff. There are so many products and services out there on the market today to show you how to build websites, but very few of them show you how to actually get traffic to your site or how to build your website so it attracts traffic.

This is important about article marketing and your WordPress blog. We've been building an Internet sales funnel using a blog in the root of your site. Some of you who have been trying to build an online business for a while already have forty-five to fifty different products. You've been working the business over the years and you are off in a million directions. I'm trying to show you how to focus in a single direction. Putting your site into a form that you can develop into a long-term business will mean you have to pick a topic and a direction.

If you would like to join our community and find out about live

webinars and have the kind of training and resources I'm

discussing in this book, get signed up for notifications at

http://www.Internetsalesfunnel.com

I will start with an example. Let's meet a very interesting lady. I think she's in her 80s. I met her a few years ago at a conference up in Calgary, Canada, but she lives in England. She has a stomach problem. It took her years to find a solution, but she found an aloe drink that works for her ailments. It has come out on the market recently and it works miracles for her. Since she started drinking this aloe juice, she's doing much, much better. So what I'm trying to get her to focus on now is "paying it forward" ("Paying it Forward" means taking something that helped you and passing it on to someone else to help them). She got started with telling the world about this cure, but did not go far enough. She hasn't figured out how to buy the products herself. She could stock and distribute the more obscure aloe products, not just the aloe juice. There is a lot to write about aloe. If you think about all the different things that aloe vera does, the history of it, how it's use spread around the world, how it is added into different products, the people that discovered it, and the medicine behind it - it is just amazing. She has a niche and a perfect business model. It is time to find the actual products to sell and tell her story. While she's at it, she might as well make an income from it. These are some of the things that we're going to be talking about.

What are you interested in? What is your topic? Do you have hobbies? How do you spend your time when you have time to burn? It is possible to monetize just about anything from maple syrup to golf carts. This book isn't about choosing that topic but if you need help with deciding, there is a free webinar available on http://www.Internetsalesfunnel.com. Just like the lady from England, there must be something that you are interested in that maybe you wondered, "How can I make money doing that?" Let's find out together. For that, you'll have to come find me online. It starts with that website.

Let's recap what we've talked about so far. What is a sales funnel? A sales funnel in its general form is primarily a WordPress blog. It has a squeeze page or multiple squeeze pages, but essentially one squeeze page with variations. We also have either articles in our blog or folders with HTML pages describing lots of different products each with a payment button. We also have an autoresponder so we can start building our list of prospects. That is all wonderful, but we want to learn how to add the right kinds of articles. How do we load our blog so it attracts traffic? Your blog has the ability to have as many articles as you want. For each one of these articles, we will do the proper SEO work (search engine optimization) in the right order. We will get listed in Google's Blog Search engine. We will install and use a WordPress SEO plugin and we will also get indexed in Google's regular search. These methods will get our site indexed in both Google search engines, the blog search engine and the regular Google search engine.

Most websites do not have this, but you will. Typical websites may have four or five pages, but you will have many. Every page you write will have SEO work done on it properly. You just have to enter the SEO elements into the fields provided. Blogs are infinitely better at picking up organic traffic off the Internet than any other type of site. Organic traffic is free, isn't it? The more articles you do, the more free traffic you bring in to your site. The more free traffic you bring in to your site, the more sales you make. I'm from California so I can say this. This is very *cool*, isn't it?

WORDPRESS AS A SITE BUILDER VERSUS OTHER SITE BUILDERS

WordPress is infinitely better than other site builders. Maybe you have never considered WordPress as a site builder. It certainly is. What is a site builder? A site builder is software you can install on a website very easily to build a very sophisticated website without much technical experience. It does not take an engineer to install or build a WordPress website. Almost anybody can learn how to use one fairly easily. Other site builders do not have the SEO capabilities. Joomla, for example, is a great tool, but Joomla is just a site builder. Godaddy's sites come with site builders too. Many companies provide some kind of site builder software that makes building your site easy, but none of them provide the RSS feeds and news capabilities of WordPress. Joomla is very cool for building a site, but it does not have the blog search capabilities, the plugins, and everything that WordPress has. WordPress in my opinion has more capabilities than Joomla and every other site builder, especially in its ability to pick up traffic. WordPress is just a completely different animal.

WordPress allows people who may not have much technical expertise and people who are not tech-savvy to be able to create articles and build a site like my sales funnel quite easily. WordPress is open source. Open source means the software that is WordPress is written by people with a lot of technical background and it is all done for *free*. You do not have to pay for a copy of WordPress. So it is made by us, for us, for our purposes.

WHAT ABOUT OTHER TRAFFIC SOURCES?

I am hoping that you are going to understand by the time we're done with this presentation that Article Marketing my way is not going to be your only source of traffic to your website. Your efforts should be well rounded using all traffic methods and everything in-between. The difference is that my brand of Article Marketing is about how you get *free* traffic. Everything else is paid traffic. You can buy traffic all day long but, if you are like me, you want as much free traffic as you can possibly get. You should be able to get thirty-five to forty-five percent of your traffic, or even higher, over a period of time from what I am teaching. In a well-rounded traffic generation marketing effort, thirty-five percent or higher of all your traffic coming from your article marketing efforts is desirable.

CREATING CONTENT

Most people do not like creating content and often think they do not have any new ideas or anything to contribute. Is that you? You might think your products or services are boring. Well, yes they probably are, but I'm always amazed at how fantastic some of these products that you see on a daily basis are made to look. You read, "Oh, my. It is the biggest secret since sliced bread," and then you visit the site, maybe give up your email address, and it is, "Oh, so what?" I hate that. You do not have to lie to people. You do not have to be sensational or make fantastic claims or anything else. If it is your topic, it is informational, and it is the truth, people are going to visit. They are looking for the information you should be providing so you do not have to be boring or sensational.

As we go through this book, I'm going to show you how to link all your products and your topics together so that you have an almost unlimited amount of content on any topic that you are talking about. You can go crazy with it. Really, if your products and services are boring now, they will be exciting. How is that for over-selling it? None of this thinking 'this is boring' stuff is true if you know where to look and where to find the content you need. There is content out there - tons and tons of content.

TRAFFIC AND LINKS

Traffic and links are critical to an understanding of what the Internet is all about. Here's a long explanation. Let's start with links. Links are defined as a clickable word or phrase that, if clicked, will bring the reader to another page. There are many kinds. There is first, second, and third tier links, offsite links, onsite links, reciprocal links and more. There are people that link to your site from their website. There are people that link back to the people that you link back to. There are people that link to the link to the link back to you. Search engines like Google, Bing, and sites like Alexa.com use links as a way of quantifying your rank among all the other sites on the Internet. Website ranking is based in large part by how many and what kind of links you have. It is also based upon traffic numbers. *The basic understanding you need is that links and traffic primarily govern your page ranking.* If your pages ranks better than another site, the thinking among search engine experts is that the search engines will send you more traffic than sites that do not rank well. A lot of people will tell you they know for certain how the search engines will rank you, but how it is done exactly changes constantly. What I have taught is basic and probably won't change anytime soon.

For the purposes of this book, you need to realize that if you are always linking to someone else's pages, then you are helping someone else's ranking. For example, let's say your site is five sites away, each site linking to each other, five tiers deep. A search engine comes along attempting to rank your site. (It is what you might call a "Web Crawler".) It keeps following the links and finally ends up on the final site. The search engine now knows who provided the original information. That site is the end of the line, the source eternal. What

I'm saying is that you want your site to be the source of that information as often as possible. The content, the patterns of keyword phrases the search engines look for, is what brings you the traffic and the links and ultimately the rankings.

It takes time to get these kinds of links, but they occur over time on their own if you follow what I teach. You have to use your imagination here. Computers housed at search engine companies have the software that *crawl* your sites. They don't care about the pictures and can't enjoy any of the wonderful videos humans like to watch. To them, it is just words and patterns and it is just content. The search engines are constantly looking for new patterns and readjusting their indexes based upon content. They are like greedy word eaters thirsty for content patterns. That is *why content is king and always will be king*. My job is to make it easy and effective as possible for you to feed these engines what they want.

Let me give you another visual of what a search engine's world might be like. A friend's website has been around for many years. This person has other websites, but brands the site using her name. If you took a look at all the people that have linked back to her site over the years, it would look like the biggest, craziest, oak tree. There are little bitty branches with leaves and everything else hanging off of it. It is a maze of brain neurons and the craziest jumble of interconnected links that you have ever seen in your entire life. That is a small example. How about other sites like Microsoft's website? That site alone probably accounts for half of a percent of all the links on the Internet. That is even crazier to visualize in your mind. A very large percentage of websites on the Internet have reasons to link to a page somewhere on Microsoft's website. Whether it is information about a fix to a bug or where to download a patch or a new product, almost all software that runs on any version of Microsoft Windows has some involvement with Microsoft. Think about how that is linked across the Internet and it boggles the mind.

Search engines and sites like Alexa.com grade you on links as well as traffic. They grade you on how much traffic you have, and how much traffic you get from the links. If links seem to always point back to you, and the subject matter is about you and your topic, then you become the source of authority on the Internet. This is what we're after. It is what I call *Web Authority.*

You want Google and all the rest of the search engines to realize that your website is the place where everybody is getting their information. "The Source", so to speak, is what search engine crawlers are looking for. If you were a search engine web crawler computer, you are really just a piece of software running on a machine on the Internet somewhere trying to decide how to index all these billions of websites. You as the *web crawler* software are actually running on many, many machines, doing many, many jobs. You are digging through the billions of websites looking at all these pages. You cannot see the graphics. You cannot interpret the graphics or most of the HTML, nor do you care. You do not care about anything else but the words and patterns of words which are keyword phrases. (Go to any page using your browser, right-click anywhere on the page, and click *view source.* The gobbledygook you see is what the search engines see.) You follow every link you find and you have just a few nanoseconds to do this work. Based on your assessment, you index the website. Are you getting the picture yet?

So, to recap, if you wrote an original article and lots of people have linked back to you as the authority, these people are essentially saying, "If you want more information, go here." Visit this guy's site. That is where I got the information. You are the writer, the author, and the authority. Do you see that? This is the key to getting top rankings.

How do you achieve *Web Authority*? The quick answer is *content*, lots and lots of content. How often should you add content to your site? If you could do one a week, I'd say for the majority of people that would be absolutely tremendous. If you could do two articles a week I think your site would go crazy within a short period of time. The more quality content you provide the better.

PROVIDING CONTENT

Providing content and becoming the *Web Authority* is based upon the ability to write a post in your blog by finding the keyword phrase that gets the most traffic and does not have much competition from other sources. One has to do a little research for that to happen.

We will go through all of that soon. So, here's the secret again. Find the keyword phrase first. That keyword phrase will become your article title. You are going to use it a couple of times in the body of the article. It is going to be in your blog tags, which are keywords. It is going to be in the title description and keywords of the SEO plugin that you have.

Doc Stone Tip: Choose the keyword first! Write the article based upon the keyword phrase and you will pick up a certain amount of traffic with each article you write. How much traffic? That really depends on the keyword phrase and how much competition is out there using that phrase. That is why you do a little bit of research and find something without much competition, but a lot of traffic. The more of those you can find the better. If you did that once a week and you picked up a thousand hits a week, how much traffic would you have in a year? It is a lot of traffic, isn't it? And it is all free traffic, absolutely free traffic. And it is no pipe dream.

One word of advice, I keep saying one article a week. That is because it is a *minimum*. Remember I said you will be adding keyword phrases in two places. One is called tags, which is for Google's Blog Search Engine. If you do not write at least one article a week, Google's Blog Search engine will forget you exist really fast. It could be looked at as a problem, or it could be looked at as an advantage. It quickly weeds out all the lazy people and allows newcomers easy and fast entry into this search engine.

Something weird happens on the Internet. As your traffic grows it does not grow proportionately or exponentially. Traffic grows a little today, and a little bit more tomorrow, and it is fairly even at first. As you get more traffic, you get more traffic, and you get more and more traffic, and you get more and more and more traffic. As you near the goal of becoming an Authority site, the traffic becomes quite heavy. So after a year or more, if you keep this up, it is amazing the transformation. The reason for this phenomenon is that as your page ranking increases, as more sites link back to you, as your traffic increases, the search engine notice and send you more traffic than they did before.

Don't Try Tricks

It is wonderful to have absolutely great content all the time. But the truth is that not all of us are great writers. That is ok. Be aware that these web crawler computers really haven't got a clue if what you wrote makes sense to a human. True artificial intelligence is still a long way off. These computers do not understand higher human thoughts. You could try and trick these computers as many people do with gobbledygook, micro fonts, and whatever trick you can think of. I do not suggest you do that. For one thing, real people do come to your site and take a look at it, and may say, "What in the world is this?" You are not going to sell anything that way. Another reason is that you do not know what Google has up its sleeves. Every day, they are making new strides into knocking cheaters off the net. You might get away with it for a while, but someday - probably sooner than you think - your site will suddenly become invisible. Use your common sense. Play the game fairly and you will never go wrong. The bottom line is that you want to have some real content. Do not take shortcuts. Try to be the best writer you can and that will be good enough. You will get better the more you practice. On the other hand, later I will reveal a number of sources where you can get the content you need for very little money.

What Is Content For The Writer?

What is *content* to you? For a search engine, it is just a webpage that has words on it that needs to be indexed. For you, the author, it's a work of art that you created. For the visitor, its information they need. These pages need text, a minimum of 250 words but usually over 400 words are better. The maximum is what you need to write the article and make it complete. If it gets too long, split it up into multiple articles.

What about duplication? Some article marketing sites require absolutely original, never before published material. These days, so does Google. If an article marketing directory site does not require original content, they probably are not worth the trouble. There are tools out there that allow you to spin an article called *Spinners*. This software allows you to submit an article and it will *spin it* and give you twenty different versions of the same text. Most of these versions of your original article are completely unreadable and worthless. You could try and fix them I suppose, but the gist of an article has a beginning, middle, and an end, and if you start spinning it too much it is useless. If you are going to spin, you should spin no more than two or three different ways. You can spin them on your own without the use of spinner. Article Marketing sites like ezinearticles.com require you to have an absolutely original article and they verify it. Google will ding you if it finds any duplication or what they consider plagiarism. Is originality important? Yes, originality is important. I said you *could* spin the article but do so at your own risk. Fortunately, you have this book. I will show you how to not to worry about what to write.

CONTENT CURATION

Let me cover quickly a concept called content curation before we discuss creating content. Curation is essentially a form of borrowing. Curation is taking old articles you find on the Internet about your subject or topic that are outdated and no longer pertinent and bringing them forward, making them current, and making them your own. This one idea alone will give you almost an unlimited amount of content for your site. Here is an example. This particular course that I'm teaching is quite a few years old. I had to teach from a group of specific classes for someone I worked for. As I kept teaching, I noticed it was outdated. A lot of it was very good, but things have changed. If you followed those trainings today, a lot of it would get you in trouble with the search engines. It eventually morphed into what you are reading today. There is very little of the original material remaining. It is brought forward to today's standards including my own thought processes and integrated into an overall traffic generation plan.

We have all learned most of what we know from someone else whether it was from a book or in a class. A lot of us learned things on our own and added it to what we read or were taught. It became our opinions and what we believed. Everybody teaches a little bit differently. If you are teaching something, make it your own. Use your own wordings. Reteach or rewrite using your own understanding. If you do this, you should never get in trouble. Change things up a bit more to accomplish what should be and is considered original.

Content curation is taking an older article and bringing it current. It is a form of borrowing so don't copy and paste. Get the gist of the article and rewrite it on your own words. The problem some writers have is coming up with material. Content curation can be one way to help provide plenty of material.

WHAT TO WRITE

What should the article be about? It should be about the topic you chose. Let me repeat, you *have* to choose a topic. Do not do what you think everybody else is doing. Do something you like to do. In the home business Internet marketing arena, it seems everybody is trying to market the same old stuff. If you surf the typical traffic exchange or read emails from safelists, you will see fifteen people and sometimes hundreds marketing the same particular product. If you see fifteen pages of the same product on a single traffic exchange, it probably means there are hundreds, if not thousands, selling that same product. That is ok, a little competition never hurt, but it also means most of these people are selling someone else's products as an affiliate. As an affiliate, they are making very little themselves, while the product owner is cleaning up. If you take cars for example, say a Ford dealership, there are thousands of Ford dealerships and they all sell lots of cars. That is a lot of competition. It is a great big world and there are plenty of people to sell to, but those car dealerships have territories. You do not see fifteen Ford dealerships in one small town. With a good product, the competition is not as critical, but if you are unique, you just won't have that much competition. Being unique makes it a whole lot easier. Keep that in mind when you choose your topic. Just do not be so unique that nobody cares to buy anything. Remember, almost any topic will do. It is how you monetize that topic that matters. If you become part of my online family, one of the services I provide is help to figure out how to monetize a topic. If you are having trouble figuring this out - and most people do - try me.

> If you would like to join our community and find out about live
>
> webinars and have the kind of training and resources I'm
>
> discussing in this book, get signed up for notifications at
>
> http://www.Internetsalesfunnel.com

For instance, let's take the lady with the aloe vera drinks that we were talking about earlier. If she expands to all kinds of add-ons and variations, a virtual clearing house for all things aloe vera, selling the more obscure things that are hard to find, she has herself a business that will grow and survive over time. Aloe vera grows wild in Hawaii. I do not think it grows at all in England where she lives, unless it is grown inside. It probably all has to be imported to England. So how much of the importing could she do? I don't know, but I do know she could drop-ship from the manufacturers. There is a lot to know, but the point is that it is a fairly unique niche without a lot of competition.

Know your topic inside and out. Become the authority on your topic. It will happen naturally. As you continue to write articles about your subject, you rapidly really do become an authority.

HOW TO TIE IN TO YOUR TOPIC THINGS THAT DON'T TIE IN

As you are going to see, choosing a new topic does not mean that you cannot be an affiliate for a traffic exchange. It does not mean that you cannot be an affiliate for a safelist. It does not mean that you cannot be an affiliate for learning tools like Internetsalesfunnel.com or contactlistbuilder.com, or contentcuration.com for example. There are many products that you may have become involved with before you started reading this book. You may be an affiliate for quite a few products already. You don't have to stop. All of it fits, even though, for example, your topic is aloe vera. You don't have to throw these products out. Your new topic will still help you make a few commissions from these other products.

Let me give you a thought process on how to tie in this relationship, "Hey, I've been out here on the Internet for two years now, and my topic is aloe vera. Thank you for your support and patronage. Some of you have asked me how I built this business. I've been able to build this wonderful business using some great tools. One of the tools that I've been using for the last year to help me generate traffic and sell my aloe vera products is this safelist. You want more information? Please 'click here.'" The reader is taken to your affiliate page. You hopefully make a commission. The safelist is not your main business or topic. But if it indeed helped you get where you are, you should tell people. Why shouldn't you make a little money telling people how you built your business? Do you understand what I'm saying? The point is that you do not have to stop selling what you already may be selling. You just look at it differently and tie it to your main topic.

IS THERE ROOM FOR YOU?

We will be looking at the Google AdWords keyword tool, and other tools to find keyword phrases with high search volume and low competition. Search engines love content. Content comes from writers like us. That is something that they cannot provide on their own. We provide it. They eat it up. They want the best and they do compare your work with other sites. Just remember, we are learning some secrets, good secrets, white hat secrets, keep Google happy secrets. These will help us get ahead of our competition. There are still many, many areas on the Internet that are uninhabited. There is still plenty of room for you.

Where are you now?

Where are you now? Maybe you have one website with three or four straight HTML pages. One of them is your index.html default page. That is the main page. Hopefully it has at least title, description, and keyword Meta tags. (Remember, we discussed the TDK, Title, Description, and Keywords?) Are you really expecting get ranked highly in the search engines this way? Understand what I'm saying. You will be paying for all your advertising unless you make some changes. This is why your blog is so important. WordPress blogs can have many articles, each one ranking for a keyword phrase. That means in a year's time, if you write an article a week, you will have fifty-two articles. In two years you will have one hundred and four. In addition to writing the article, you have to do the TDK, the Title, Description and Keywords for every single page that you do in order to get ranked. That site with four or five pages done as well as you can, will not compare to a WordPress site with fifty two pages. Do you see the difference? I have described a path for you to follow. You know where you are now. Make a plan now to transform your site from where it is to where you know you need to be.

TELL THE SEARCH ENGINES YOU EXIST

One more thing; do not forget to tell the search engines you exist. So many websites exist that are using every black hat trick in the book to attract traffic. Some are so bad, they are considered spam websites. In order to combat these types of websites, Google and Bing have provided what is called Webmaster tools. These tools allow you to tell the search engines you exist and you are not a spam site. They will take a look at your site with their webcrawlers. That is the way it is these days. You must tell the major search engines you exist and are legitimate or they may not bother to take a look at all. If you haven't done so, plan on visiting http://www.google.com/webmasters and http://www.bing.com/toolbox/webmaster and do what they tell you to do.

CONTENT ATTRACTS KEYWORDS

Content attracts keyword phrase searches. Pages create page rank. More pages create more page ranking power and that is why blogs are so important. Put your blogs in the root of your primary top website. That is the whole crux of this entire Internet Sales Funnel model. I know it is simple, but it is so important. Content is a little bit like money. Its money that you could have spent on paid advertising. It is worth your time.

Let's use an example. Meet George. George has a blog where he's selling WordPress plugins. If George had a blog and every week he wrote an article using a new keyword phrase that had something to do with the plugins that he's selling, he would begin to bring a little bit more website traffic with each one of these pages. Each week, George should write about one of the features of one of the plugins; why it works and why it works so well for each plugin. He should spotlight a problem that this feature solves knowing that his plugin is the solution. The article solves the problem for the reader and has a link to a product page that has a link to where readers can buy the plugin. This is how you bring traffic in. Write your article so that you are not selling directly. You are pointing out a problem, discussing possible solutions, and providing your solution. Is this making sense or not?

Everybody wants content. If it is your content, you control it. The more you control, the better you rank. Since you have the content and you control it, people link back to you because they found information they were looking for. Your foot print in the Internet just keeps growing. And you always have a call to action, say, "Hey, for more information on this 'click here.'" Then hopefully your readers visit your sales pages and spend money.

CONTENT IS KING, LINKS IS QUEEN

We've talked about content and why it is king. I say, if Content is King, then "Linking is Queen." Page ranking is dependent primarily on traffic and links. They go hand in hand. You need both. Let's talk about links. Links are the beginning of all traffic. The links from search engines link to websites like yours. Get good at making links. Create links between pages on your own site and links from pages on other sites. Even if you have multiple sites, link back to your own pages. Create links from social sites - Facebook, Twitter, Pinterest, Google Plus, and LinkedIn - all of them. Always leave links from comments you make on other people's sites. All links are valuable, but some are more valuable than others. When we're done, we will lay out what the best kinds of links are and how to get them.

LAZY LINKING

Let me give you an example of what kind of lazy black hat practices are being used to create links to people's sites. If you have ever created a WordPress blog, you've seen these kinds of links already and maybe did not realize where they come from. Remember all that spam you get in your blog that shows up as comments and drives you crazy? It is constant and won't go away. You should have an Akismet plugin pre-installed in your blogs. Hopefully you have it activated. It is there to combat spam. Every one of these spam comments has many links, sometimes as many as thirty to fifty and it's all total garbage. These links do not last long. As soon as you do a check for spam in the admin area of your blog and delete it, it is gone. Some you will recognize this spam quickly because it is obvious. The comments are sneaky. They say sickly sweet things about you and your site, but the comment is so generic, it can be used as a comment on anything. They do that because unscrupulous Internet companies sell so-called links to help promote your site. You pay them some money, then provide them a generic statement that can used as a comment on any site, then submit it. You are thinking, "Wow, I will get five thousand links for fifty bucks". The truth is that you just became a spammer. You check your backlinks in a few days and you are very happy - "Look at all those links". Within a week or two, most of your links will be gone and you just might get yourself blacklisted by Google. That is not how you get links and it is a total waste of time and money. If you see these and approve them, they will be published and visible, do not do it. That would create a permanent link for the spammer. That is what they want you to do. I bring it up because I'm going to teach you the right way to get links that stay. If you do make a comment on someone's blog, be very careful to have your comment not look to a savvy webmaster like spam. Every time you make a comment, put a link in, but say something like. "Hey, I am so and so. I read your article on such and such. I agree with you on (something specific)" or maybe you disagree. And then maybe add, "I have a lot more information on that particular subject here." Then you add your link. Most webmasters will allow that. Now you have a tier one link back to your site by a comment you made. These are great links, but still not *Web Authority* level links. Anyway, I wanted to bring that up in case you were thinking you could take the easy way to creating links.

What other kinds of links are there? There are links from JV's (joint ventures and partners) and links from Strategic Alliances (a group of site owners working together), or other people that you work with. You know, "You put a link on my site; I will put a link on your site". Maybe you've got a little flashing logo or something that your partner can use to make a link back to you. You can swap with someone. There are many variations of that kind of link. These are what we call reciprocal links. There are links from social sites. There are links we make from one of our own websites to another one of our sites or other people that link from their pages. There are links from pages inside our sites to other pages inside the same site. These are called onsite links. There are many other kinds of links, but there is one kind of link that is best in my opinion. We want a one-way link from another website not belonging to us where the trail terminates on our content. The buck stops on us. I think these are easier to get than some of the swap-type links and they are more valuable, but they require a special kind of article. They are called viral articles. I'm going to be concentrating on teaching you how to create as many of these kinds of links as you can handle the right way, the white hat way, the search engine friendly way.

Search engine and page ranking depends on links. All links are good links. Some are better than others. What do we get from these links? We get traffic from these links. Any link will provide some amount of traffic. The quality of the link is the variable. Search engines find you through your links. They may index a particular keyword phrase and be looking for the source. Let me explain how to make this link.

MAGIC LINKS

You want to use the keyword phrase as your link if at all possible. Highlight the keyword phrase words in your article and click the chain link icon in your WordPress editor. A small dialog screen will pop up. Enter the website URL where a visitor who clicked the link should be taken. It should be a related article. Hopefully it is the one you wrote with that same keyword phrase in the title. Enter the alt tag using the keyword phrase and save it. An alt tag looks like this in HTML code <alt>. The alt tag is a holdover for years ago when the Internet was so slow that some browsers could not display images. The alt tag denotes text to display instead of the image on a slow browser. It's *alternate* to the image or link. What results is that the actual website URL is not seen, only the keyword phrase is seen by your visitors. They see a blue underlined keyword phrase they can click on. That is a very strong link because a search engine will follow these links to see where they lead. If they see a link on a keyword phrase lead to an article that is related to what the keyword phrase says, it is a special kind of link. When you are making links from pages to pages within your site, and from your site to other sites, and any kind of link for that matter, create a link that incorporates the keyword phrase, it is golden.

One other word on this; do not take your visitors who click on keyword phrase magic links to a completely unrelated subject. Your visitors will not appreciate being taken to a page they don't want to see and Google won't appreciate it either. Do not overdo it by making too many of these on a single article or page either. Google will penalize you for that too. That is a form of keyword spamming.

How Writing Content Gets You Links

Content provides traffic because search engines want content. We're giving it to them. Webmasters need content for their sites too, but so many are not good at writing, refuse to write, are too lazy to write, but mostly, they do not know any better. They are lured by the easy way out. So they are happy to use anyone else's writing. Most article marketing sites are places where you can submit your articles, get them published and then re-published or syndicated. Once they are published, you and anyone else can use them on their own websites. Article marketing site user guidelines usually require the user to maintain some links. Usually they ask you to maintain two links, one link back to the article marketing site and one to the author. When someone uses your article and re-posts it to their website, you get a one way authority site link.

WHY NOT USE A 3RD PARTY CONTENT SERVICE?

Like many, if you absolutely do not want to write your own content, you might look to certain kinds of content source providers. There are services you can buy to get somebody else's content articles put on your site, sometimes manually, sometimes automatically. Some are quite pricey. You may be thinking that you will bring in all this traffic with these great articles. The problem is that it is someone else's stuff. Not only that, it is more than likely the same article will be sent to several hundred people or more. It is all duplication. Something Google hates. If that wasn't bad enough, have you ever clicked on one of these articles on a site using a typical WordPress syndication plugin for example? Guess where it takes you? It takes the reader away from your site and onto the author's site. Why would you want something like that? It is great for that original author that you just helped out and that is about it. Then there are services that send you an article you can paste in yourself and those won't take the reader away from your website, but it is still sent to hundreds of people. It is duplication again. Everybody does it and I just do not know why. About the only thing you can hope for is an occasional visitor that might visit you by accident and click on an ad. That is a terrible strategy. I think most people do this because they do not think they can write anything worthwhile or they just do not know better. Keep reading, I think you will be more than confident before this book is done.

The bottom line is that you want to write your own articles. If you need to borrow someone else's article, learn how to cure it as we've discussed earlier. Reword it, make it your own, make it so it is different enough that nobody could tell where it came from. That pretty much means reading the article or group of articles to be curated and trying to write them off the top of your head instead of copying and pasting. You will be safe this way. You have the subject. You have the topic. It is a very interesting topic. Put it in your own words. Cure it and put it in your own site. Instead of you buying other people's hard work, putting it on your site so that you can provide these other authors all your hard won traffic, why not be the one that is providing the articles for everybody else so that they can provide *you* their hard won traffic? Just remember the article you submit to a service like this as an author will end up as overly duplicated all over the Internet. If it is going to be provided as text people can paste into their sites, get a good price for your hard work. That is all you will get out of it.

WHY ARTICLE MARKETING?

Article Marketing by the old definition does not work anymore but article marketing, as I am defining it, works very well to attract traffic and links to your site. It is white hat and won't get you in trouble with the search engines. Search engines are cracking down on black hat practices. Effects from black hat tricks are almost always short lived. Sometimes the bad effects of black hat practices are permanent rejection by the search engines. Black hat practices are going away for a couple of reasons. The search engines are hip to it and they are losing money because of it. Remember the old adage, "Follow the money"? Black hat practices are attempts to attract free organic traffic away from legitimate information based websites by tricking webcrawlers into ranking their sites higher than legitimate sites. We've all seen this if you've ever spent fifteen minutes surfing. You end up on some website that has zero to do with what you were looking for that is trying to sell you male enhancement drugs or worse. If these advertisers cannot get away with these tricks anymore, they'll have to pay for their advertising like the rest of us. Google and Bing want their money. What Google and Bing are doing will ultimately pay off big too. They are almost there. Little by little, I'm seeing fewer and fewer sites that practice these black hat tricks.

What this means for legitimate sites is that if you've been a good little webmaster, obeying all the rules all this time, using clean practices, and providing clean original content, you actually are going to be rewarded with more traffic. These black hat practice people are not going to be taking all the traffic away from valid sources anymore. White hat article marketing creates the best links and these are long term permanent links.

How Long Do Links Stick Around?

Some legitimate articles that were written years ago are still around. I heartily encourage you to stop fooling around with here today, gone tomorrow products and start working on a long term business as a real entrepreneur. One good reason is that as you build your business, the Internet works with you if you know what you want to accomplish. For example, links that refer back to your site might be out there for many years. There is no other kind of advertising that can work for you longer than even a few months unless you are an old magazine in a doctor's office. You cannot get better advertising than this. If you pay to put an ad in a magazine, how much do you spend on it? That magazine may sit on a doctor's office waiting room table for a month or two or it might get to someone who will thumb through it and throw it away, but the effect doesn't last very long.

TV ads are in existence for fifteen to thirty seconds, and then they are gone. You have to pay for it again if you want someone to see it again. I'm not saying that TV, mailers, and magazines do not work. They do and they have their place. What I am saying is a page on the Internet with a link back to you is almost permanent. As a matter of fact, there are more and more sites out on the Internet that need to be removed. The site is still hosted but nobody belongs to the site. I often come across companies that are out of business and have been for a while. Their websites will still sell you their software.

I recently went online to buy some very specialized SQL synchronization software. I found five different pieces of software that might work. Out of five companies, only one of them was still in business. I had to take a look at some of the blog entries that people had written that said, "I do not think they are here anymore." And they weren't. That is how permanent some of the advertising the Internet provides can be. It might even outlive you.

How To Succeed And Fail At Article Marketing

Getting the right kind of links is what article marketing on article marketing websites and directories is all about. We will get more detailed about this later, but for now, try and remember that there are three kinds of articles - product articles, informational articles, and viral articles. The only types of articles I suggest you have published in article marketing directories are the viral kind. These produce links. Viral articles being re-published are the best kind and they are easier to get I think than any other way. This next section pertains to getting links, not to getting traffic. It will focus on article marketing to article marketing websites and directories using viral articles. We will delve deeper into what a viral article is and how to write one, but first let's talk about getting them published.

Most people get article marketing wrong, but you are not going to. It is simple to do this kind of marketing once you know how. It is not a big deal to get this right. You have already made the right move by reading this book. Most of what I'm telling you involves writing four hundred word or more articles and publishing them. You will publish some in article marketing sites and some on your blog. I will show you how to do all of that. It is easy. It is also easy and inexpensive to outsource the writing and still be totally white hat. You can even have other people do it for you and it costs you next to nothing. Of course, if you do the writing yourself, it costs nothing at all except your time. And it works at massive scales. You could go as big as you want to with this. It is a great branding vehicle to make a name for yourself and for whatever products that you are carrying. It is the right way to go.

Let's talk about how you can fail in your marketing efforts as a writer. Write a boring article, a self-serving article, with a link to your website. Submit it to an article marketing site. Usually these sites require an original never before published article. Do not write it in your blog if you are going to submit it for publishing. Use a word processor first. There are requirements and guidelines to follow for each site. Usually you have to maintain a link back to the article directory and one to yourself. Sounds easy so far, right?

Once you have submitted the article to a directory and it has been accepted, you will now have one of these coveted links we want. Next, you find another directory and submit that same article. Now you have another link from a second directory. You can repeat this until you run out of article marketing sites and directories. There are even services that allow you to submit it to fifty or more article marketing directories at once for you. It is all automatic and inexpensive. This gives you fifty awesome links. What is wrong with that? Well, nothing's wrong with that. But, if you are expecting traffic from it, and you want to get some sales from it, there is a lot wrong with submitting to fifty directories that nobody ever visits. There are only a small number of large directories that people bother to visit. Which ones are the biggest is changing every year too. At the outset, this seems great in that we now have a bunch of links from a bunch of article marketing directories and all links are good. Well - not necessarily. As I said, you won't get much from this method.

Let's talk about how to succeed. Write an article that other people want to read. Write an article that other webmasters might want to re-publish for their own sites. What do other people and other webmasters want? They want the kind of article that is not the kind you normally have in your blog. You might put it in your blog eventually, but you are not writing this article for your blog. The article can be quite unrelated to your topic. We hope it is very viral. It might be funny. This is an article that other readers are interested in, not what you are interested in. You then have it published. The reason for writing an article like this is to get links back to your website. This in turn increases your page ranking. You may not actually get much traffic from these kinds of articles. That is ok. We're looking for the links. The end result is that you submitted your article to one directory and now you have a link from that directory. That is it. You are all done.

Ten days later, if it is a great article, maybe four websites have re-published or "syndicated" your article - not article marketing directories but other websites - other webmasters. According to guidelines for other webmaster to use your published articles, they must maintain a link back to you, the author. Now you have four, absolutely great, level one, most highly desired links from other webmasters. A month later there is a dozen links from as many sites, same kind of links. This keeps growing over time. It is a totally different way of thinking.

Think about what other people want not what you want. Eskimos in Alaska are not going to buy many ice cubes, for example. I just read a great book about the horse Seabiscuit. The story began in 1906 when the earthquake hit in San Francisco and the city fell down. The eventual owner of Seabiscuit had a Buick automobile dealership. For years, he couldn't sell many cars. After the earthquake hit, every car was sold in just a few days. You couldn't get horses around the town due to the rubble and there was nothing for the horses to eat. People were eating the horses. There was plenty of gasoline and people discovered you could get around quickly in a car. You have to think about what other people want when they need it, not what you want.

We've discussed failure versus success. As you have seen, directory links from directories do not matter. They are just the intermediary. You submit to directories, but the goal is to get our articles re-published or syndicated. Only the very few best directories matter. Traffic and ranking these sites will tell us which is best. You can look this up on http://www.alexa.com for example. Great content is always the key to a great publishable article. As long as people love to read interesting and fun articles, this will never fail. The content you write is not about you. It is not about the directories. It is about the consumer. The consumer is other webmasters that need content for their sites. The bottom line is to get something published you think might go viral in the biggest article marketing directory you can find.

Is this making sense yet? This is my definition of how article marketing gets these links we need. Links are just one part of it though. Remember I said there are three kinds of articles that you will need to write for your site? This kind of article marketing is the link side of an overall traffic strategy. Articles do cost time and sometimes money if you hire writers, but all links cost time or money, don't they? Paid links are fixed, but cost money - lots of money. And they require you to put money in periodically. Reciprocal links are hugely time-consuming and they do not rank quite as well. An example of a reciprocal link might be that I would give you a link on my site and you give me a link on your site. You have to double check reciprocal links periodically to make sure the link is still there. We may have to talk or email several times back and forth as well. Nothing works quite as well as writing a viral article, submitting it to a large article marketing directory and letting the links come to you.

Bookmarking and social site links like facebook and twitter can provide links as well. It is cheap and easy to get these kinds of links. But these have limited ranking benefits compared to level one links from other sites linking back to you.

Buying links like I described earlier that create comments in people's blogs is called spam. It is trash and it will disappear in a week. These spam services will hurt your rankings. Do not buy these services. It is computer generated junk. You might buy into one of these services, and say, "Wow, look at all the links I have." In two weeks, everybody will clear their spam and you won't have any links anymore. It is a waste of time and money.

Articles done right are always better and they only have a one-time cost. The linking is broadly distributed, and if you get it to go viral, you get a lot of links quickly. Getting something to go viral will put you on the Internet map, so to speak. I know people who are making a very good living just off of YouTube ads because of the types of viral videos they are able to create. You need some talent for some of these videos, but just a little will go a long way for our purposes. You do not have to have that much talent to get something to go viral just a little. We're not looking to make a living off one video; but we do want a few great links each time we write a viral article we get published.

WHAT IS VIRAL?

You must know what I mean by viral. We all do this. We get emails or facebook posts and it is funny or really interesting, or really cute or even really gross, and you pass it on to your friends. Then your friends pass it on to their friends. Then your friend's friends pass it even further down the line. Something really viral can go around the world in just days. That is why they call it viral. It started out sent to one or several people. Somehow it is passed on worldwide all on its own.

For something to go viral, it obviously has to be something that people will pass on. You must all see these emails we get from friends quite often? They are jokes, pictures, stories, and videos. What would you pass on? What would you not pass on? Think about it. Keep thinking about it. Links derived from articles like this will have a direct page ranking benefit. Your articles then become assets. Content is the investment, links are the dividend. Article cost divided by links is the measure. Some articles will perform better than others, but they are all better than the alternatives. That is enough for now about links and viral articles.

MAXIMIZING SYNDICATION

Let's discuss syndication. First, what is syndication? For our purposes, it is publishing an article to an article marketing directory website. When another webmaster sees the article and wants to use it, they can re-publish it on their own website and it becomes part of their own content. The webmaster that uses the article must maintain a link back to you as the original author. Once it is re-published, the article is essentially syndicated. We're going to be discussing how to maximize this re-publishing or syndication.

Second, how does one get an article that you published used by other webmasters so you get as many awesome links as you can? Remember, we need both traffic and links to increase and maintain our page ranking with the search engines. Syndication helps pull in those links and hence it helps increase page ranking.

There are a couple of different kinds of articles you could publish to accomplish that. Each will have different results, but each involves getting a good original article that has never been published accepted by an article marketing directory site first. We're not talking about one of those automated article marketing services that submits your article to fifty or sixty useless sites for a one dollar. We're talking about getting the article published on one of the top five article marketing sites on the Internet. Once you get it published on the article marketing directory, we want it syndicated by other webmasters who will use it as part of their own content. When they use it, they have to provide a link back to you as the author. They also have to provide a link back to the article marketing site. That is usually the bare minimum requirement of the submission guidelines of article publishing. Restated, instead of you being somebody that goes out to an article marketing site to borrow articles to use on your site and providing a link back to the original author, you are providing the articles to other website owners who do not want to write. You are the content, instead of buying the content. Instead of you essentially doing some marketing for that other author, they are marketing for you. As you can tell, there are advantages to being the author who is syndicated, rather than doing the syndication.

I related this before. On a number of these syndication websites, there is software you can buy for quite a sum that has a built in syndication plugin. It seems an awesome thing. The webmaster does not have to write any of their own content and the website will be packed full of great articles. It gives a new marketer all of these really well-done articles to use. In some cases, the articles are automatically posted for you. That seems just wonderful from the outside looking in. The thing is though, if a visitor to your site clicks anywhere in the body of the article, the visitor is taken to original author's blog. Not all do this, but some do. As a newbie, you do not know any better. As a newbie, you take all the time and trouble and money to bring some traffic to your site just to get the visitors to look at the ads they have on the sidebar. If the visitor accidentally or intentionally clicks on the article, they end up on the original author's site and no longer on your site. So, do you want to be the person who is marketing for the author, or do you want to be the author and have other people do the marketing for you?

SUMMARY

Having others do some of your marketing is a great reason to write articles like this, but the other reason is for the author links. These are level one links, the best kind of links you can get. Somebody has used your article, put it on their site and there is a link back to you as the end of the line. No matter how many times the article gets syndicated and re-published, if the search engines follow the links, they will end up on your site. You are the one with the knowledge. You are the one with the original article. You are creating your own *Web Authority*. What we're trying to do is maximize the number of times that our article gets re-published. We're providing the content for someone else and they are doing some of the marketing for us. It helps take the cost of the article and spread it out over as many links as possible, minimizing the cost and maximizing our exposure.

SELECTING ARTICLE MARKETING DIRECTORIES

You want to select directories you want to use, but you only need a couple. You only need the biggest and best ones. They are not that hard to get published in, but there are a few guidelines to follow. What happens when we utilize multiple directories? Even just three directories make us consider what is called sequencing. When it comes to article marketing, sequencing refers to knowing what each article marketing directory guidelines require of us and figuring out the best way to accomplish getting the article published in these directories so we do not break any rules. For example, the first directory we want to submit to requires an absolutely original article that has never been published anywhere else. If you want to get published in that particular directory, you have to let it get published there first. Some of the other article directory sites may not have as stringent of a requirement. Once it is published, if you want to use it again, you can. That does create duplication. Because of that, I am going to add a great big caution. What I suggest is just one article marketing directory or one dedicated to your topic or genre and that is it. I use EzineArticles.com. If you still want to try two or more directories, you could try re-wording the article so it is still yours and still original, but make it different enough so that it won't be seen as duplication. That can be dangerous if you do not re-word it substantially. If you follow my advice, you will only need one or maybe two versions of the article anyway. Sequencing just means; this one's got this requirement, that one's got that requirement, and another has some other requirement, and what is the best way to make them all happy? In other words, what are the steps that I have to do, and in what order do they have to be made to make the articles directories happy?

SELF SYNDICATION

There is the concept of self-syndication. That is just using your article on your own site. This is an important distinction because an overall strategy for marketing your site will use articles that will be published and some that will be content only for your site. We will cover the different types of articles we will need in more depth later.

Other than this term "self-syndication", meaning you are publishing yourself, there is no need to consider this concept any further.

DIRECT SYNDICATION

Direct syndication is the idea of cutting out the article marketing directories altogether and going direct to the webmasters that need content. If you write a lot and do it well, some webmaster may contact you to see if you would contribute articles on their site. It is worthwhile to get a link back to your site if the site has a fair amount of traffic. Again, use Alexa.com to determine how much traffic the site is really getting. If you see a good blog with a whole lot of traffic, especially if the topic fits you in both style and topic, you can contact them or write a comment in their blog as an ice-breaker that basically says, "Hi, I really like your blog, I'd like to help contribute to the content of your site." Set up an arrangement with them but make sure there is still an author block or resource box providing that link for you. If you can find websites with a lot of traffic and great content, and you become a contributor for them, while they maintain a link back to you, you have cut out the article directory site altogether. You may not make it a priority, but you will come across them in your travels on the Internet. The opportunities are out there. Direct syndication is bypassing the article marketing directories themselves and going direct to the webmaster that needs the content. One last thing on this subject; if they do not want to maintain a link, and you still want to write for them, you should charge accordingly. If they do not maintain a link to you without "nofollow" or pay you for your services, there will be no value to you. (The term "nofollow" is an HTML directive to web crawlers from search engines to not follow the link to the source. Hence you will not get credit for the link as the author)

SUBMISSION GUIDELINES

Every article marketing directory site has article submission guidelines. They have their rules. You cannot get your article published unless it is an absolutely original article in most every case. I haven't seen a reputable article directory site allow duplication in a long while. If there are any other problems with your article, they will let you know after you start making submissions. Some problems might be too many links on the page, your grammar looks elementary school level, poor quality content, white space, and the list goes on. It seems it is always something. You will catch on and start writing properly shortly. Its good practice and they will help you.

Most of the problems they point out are common sense and the guidelines are common across most sites. If you can afford to upgrade on some of these article directory sites, they are more relaxed with the rules, but I would suggest you stay as a free author until you get 10 or more articles published.

USING THE ARTICLES ON AN ARTICLE MARKETING WEBSITE

An article marketing directory site has thousands of articles my many authors. These sites are jam-packed full of content. What if you would like to use the content these sites provide on your own sites instead of writing your own? It turns out you can. There are rules for that as well. I would not do it. There is very little benefit to you in the way of traffic or links. It is not exactly duplication if you do it right. They provide some HTML code that makes this possible, but why bother. If you use other people's content, it means most of your traffic must come from other sources like paid traffic or has some other form of built-in traffic. It means you do not need the links. If you are trying to get traffic to your site for free as I am teaching you to do in this book, stay away from the duplication and perceived duplication. We want that link. That is what we as authors are hoping for.

Fortunately there are still a lot of webmasters that want to use other people's content. There are also still a lot of webmasters that haven't gotten the message about duplication yet. There are a lot of webmasters that have built-in traffic too. The rules for reusing an article, for example, require you to maintain a link to the site that did the publishing. That is you, the author. There is a different set of rules for authors and for webmasters wanting to use the article on their own sites. Be aware of both and make sure the site you use allows both.

ARTICLE MARKETING DIRECTORY SELECTION CRITERIA

If you are writing health related content for example, there are article marketing sites that are almost all health related. There are sites that are just Internet marketing related. There are a lot of different kinds of sites that an author can submit an article. If you have unique content, you will be looking for one of those directories that have the same kind of unique content that you are writing about. These topic-related sites have topic restrictions. In the case of the health related site, they do not want anything else. If all you do is health related content, then your directory selection will be limited. Match the directory to the topic.

Traffic is also a huge criterion when selecting a directory. Get the website URL, go out to http://www.alexa.com and paste the websites you want to check in the field provided. If you have four or five article marketing directories to choose from, figure out which one has the big, bigger, and biggest amount of traffic.

Another thing to consider when you are looking at these different directories is what kind of traffic analytics do they provide you? Can they provide details on the number of impressions and clicks and their associated ratios for you?

Note: An impression is when the opportunity to click a link appears but nobody clicks it. The ratio between impressions and clicks would mean the percentage of times an ad must appear before it gets clicked.

Do they provide you any kind of demographics? What kind of information can they provide? This may not seem that important now, but later as you develop a product and a sales funnel that is working, you really do need to know just exactly who your market is. The more you know about the kind of person that actually makes a purchase from you, the more efficient your dollars will be when you spend them for paid advertisements.

TOP ARTICLE MARKETING DIRECTORY SITES

The website http://www.ezinearticles.com has been one of the biggest directories around for these last few years. This is one that requires an absolutely original article be submitted.

Other sites that warrant mention are:

http://www.goarticles.com

http://www.articlesnatch.com

http://www.articledashboard.com

http://www.articlealley.com.

Other notable sites would be:

http://www.hubpages.com

http://www.sooperarticles.com

http://www.articlebase.com and

http://www.selfgrowth.com.

Check these out yourselves. Do not take this list as the last word. At the writing of this book, it is a good list, but things change. It should help you get started though. I mostly write on ezinearticles.com and once in a while, I will use one of the others. For the kind of overall strategy I am writing about in this book, you really only need the biggest article marketing directory you can find. Please note that a site like SelfGrowth.com is about self-growth. That topic is limited and they are probably not going to want to know about Internet marketing techniques.

WHAT KINDS OF ARTICLES SHOULD YOU SUBMIT?

This book is about making your site an authority site and commanding as much of the traffic in your niche as possible. In order to do that, you need an overall strategy that incorporates attracting one-way links and lots of traffic from many kinds of sources. Most of the articles you write will probably be written for publishing or self-syndication on your own blog. The ones to submit to article marketing directories are the ones that have the potential of going viral and attracting those links we've been discussing. Selecting a directory with the most traffic is really all you need. Feeding those articles that have the potential of going viral or at least have the potential to attract webmasters to syndicate them is all we need to submit. The rest of the articles we will write will be for immediate publishing into our blog. Using this philosophy allows you to avoid the entire argument and problems associated with duplication and duplicate content that the search engines look for.

MORE ON SEQUENCING

Let's discuss a little more about sequencing multiple directories. Let's say we want to submit to two different directories. You submit to EzineArticles.com first and wait for it to be published. Do one at a time. It may take a week or more if you make mistakes they ask you to fix. Once that first one is published, you decide to submit a variation of it to SooperArticles.com. You only need a few variations anyway. If you use my method, you only need the one article. Some directories allow you to re-use the very same article so in many cases you do not need to spin it. But Google does care about duplicate content so the second article may get ignored by the search engines. Why bother. If you want to submit to more than one site, you will have to do the sequencing carefully. In other words, decide which one has to be first, which one has to be second. Once you figure out the sequence with directories that you are going to work with, it will be pretty much the same thing each time. The bottom line is to make sure you meet the guidelines for that article directory.

RE-USING ARTICLES

It is so tempting to re-use the same article several times. That is why I'm spending more time on this. Should you re-use your articles? First let's define what re-using your articles really means. It means duplicating your article on more than one site. And as we have said, duplication is bad. Even so, one may argue that there are a number of places you can re-use your articles. Should you spin the article for the next directory before you re-use it? There is software that supposedly gives you many variations of the same article. Don't buy that stuff. Spin it yourself if you must spin it at all. By the time they are done spinning it, most of the versions do not make any sense. Should you also publish this same article on your own blog too? Should you let someone else use the article? You already know my answer to all of these. My answer is that you should always use an absolutely original article. Always have an original article for every purpose. Even if you later want to publish the article on your own blog and follow the directory submission guidelines which they allow, why?

The problem is not the article marketing site, it is Google. You would probably have to really get out-of-hand and try every black hat thing you could find to make your site disappear from Google's searches altogether, but the duplicate content is always going to be all but invisible. Google just ignores the duplicate content.

One last thing, ezinearticles.com, for example, has a feature for webmasters that will allow you to use the article you had published that you authored on your own blog. This is the same thing that other webmasters will use if they want to re-publish your article. They give you some HTML code for this purpose. If you must, use the HTML code they give you and go ahead and publish the article on your own site. In this way, you avoid the duplication issue. Don't expect much traffic or any links from this practice. I am suggesting you write another article.

WHAT IF YOU ABSOLUTELY JUST WANT TO USE THAT ARTICLE OVER?

Jeepers! You are persistent. What if you absolutely just want to use that article over? How much change is enough to make the article different enough to be considered no longer a duplicate? In one respect, it will depend on the submission guidelines of the directory. Better too much, than not enough. Take your article, reword it, put it in a different order or do something with it in order to make it different, but make it readable. There will be humans reading the article. And again, Google's algorithms are getting much better than they used to be for figuring out what is a duplicate and what is not. For me, I would just rather write another original article. Keep reading, there is so much to write about, I call that chapter endless content. You just do not need to duplicate anything.

PURPOSE YOUR BLOG

The purpose of writing all this content is two-fold. One is to provide something that other people will read. It has to be interesting or helpful in some way. The other is to sell your products. In order to do both, you need a good overall strategy around providing this content so you end up working smarter, not harder. Let me describe this for you quickly. You have your blog. You need some product pages in your blog. You will want to write about your products. Those are the articles or pages that are actually going to sell your product. Those pages lead directly to a payment button. You need informational articles about your topic. These bring people to your site seeking information and solutions to their problems. The solutions are the products you carry. Lastly, you need viral articles.

You are not going to publish "product articles" in an article marketing directory site. They will be strictly for publishing on your blog. Very few of your informational articles will be really worth trying to publish in an article marketing directory either. Many articles will have a limited ability to create links, but they should be good for generating traffic. Leave these product and informational articles for publishing on your own site. The last kind of article, the viral kind, is meant to be published in an article marketing directory site. Make viral articles as exciting as you possibly can with as much broad appeal. A viral article does not need to be closely related to your topic. These are the articles that we need to bring us those one way links. That is the overall strategy called for to bring in as much organic free traffic and links to your site as possible

PRODUCT ARTICLES

Product articles are the "how to use this product to help you" type article. Unless the reader is interested in acquiring the item or they have a problem this item solves, they are not going to be interested in reading them. Without these product articles, you cannot sell your product. You have to say something about the product, so that is what we call the product pages. I suggest you write at least two for every product you sell. If you are just starting out with your blog, these articles will be the first ones you need to write. They will be features and benefits and click here to buy pages.

INFORMATIONAL ARTICLES

Informational articles are articles that are on whatever the topic is on your site. We're going to be discussing what I call endless content later on in this book. We will discuss where to find plenty of content. These informational articles are what provide most of the traffic for your site. These articles should be the most fun to write because it is about a subject you chose. These will be the second type of article to add to your site if you are just starting out. Some of these informational articles could be published if they were really cool or fun, but most are just to be published to your blog using our search engine optimization secret. Find the keyword phrase first and then write the article. You should make the decision to publish the article in an article directory or just on your own blog before you write it. Once you publish it on your blog, it is no longer an original, never before published, article. Write it in a word processor offline first if you are not sure.

VIRAL ARTICLES

The last kind of article is a viral article. These are written specifically for publishing in an article marketing directory to attract webmasters to use the article and get us those links. They are not going to sell anything for us most likely. They probably won't generate that much traffic either. It will create traffic, but not directly. These are written only to generate links back to our site. By providing links, they indirectly increase our page ranking which, in turn, will increase our traffic. That is what is most important about viral articles. If somebody wants to read something more about the author, they will. And then they'll come to your site and you may have an opportunity to add them to your newsletter. Make sure where you send them in your author's resource box makes the most of that opportunity. We will discuss author resource boxes later.

PUTTING IT ALL TOGETHER

Hopefully, you are starting to understand where I'm going with all of this. Not every article you write will be published on an article marketing site. It is just certain ones with the potential to go viral or at least attract attention. The purpose of a viral article is to provide links and some small amount of traffic back to your site.

Let's discuss going viral again. Here is an example. I'm in an original rock and roll band. I have a lot of recorded original music. I can put together videos that hopefully produce some emotion in you. Maybe if that video was particularly heart-wrenching, people would pass it around, especially on Christmas or Valentine's Day for a love story. Sometimes your "viralness" can be dependent on the time of year. It may also be dependent on a new product or something happening in current events. Timing can be critical.

Since 1980, from old bulletin boards, Prodigy and AOL days, I have been collecting material that people have been passing around from one person to another. It is all viral material. Some of it is funny stuff. This includes videos, jokes, crazy music, all kinds of material. I have an incredible collection. Someday I am going to put it all together into a single video/slide show/musical. Make sure you are signed up to my list so I can send you a link when I publish it. If you pass it on, and they pass it on, etc., then it will go viral. I will make sure my author link is in my resource box.

SHOULD THE VIRAL ARTICLE LINK TO YOUR BLOG OR THE SALES PAGE?

These viral articles that you have published, or any article that you have published on an article marketing directory site, should have a link back to your site from what is called a resource box. Where would you take your readers if they are interested in you as the author and click your link? You could take them to a specific page or you could take them to a sales page. I caution you in trying to take them to any page with a payment button. The article marketing directory, if they are worth their salt, will indeed check you out. They frown on anything that sounds remotely "salesy". I suggest at a minimum, to link to a page on your blog specifically for visitors from the article marketing directory site that says something like this, "Hi, my name is Arthur Author. It is nice to have you here. I see that you must have read one of my articles out on the Internet possibly from this site or that site. I welcome you. I want to tell you what this site is about and here are some of the other links to other pages that you might be interested in. I hope you will add yourself to my list. There is a webform on the right side of the screen. Enter your name and your email in the fields provided and press the submit button."

Whatever you say, you should always have a call to action or at least ask them to add themselves to your newsletter. Once you have them on your newsletter or list, they will start receiving your emails inviting them to come and view other articles. You will have a chance to market other products to them. Remember, the purpose of the viral article is for the links, not for the traffic which will be poorly targeted. Nonetheless, people will be coming to your site to check you out. Grab them if you can.

For example, if they happen to be a wood-working hobbyist and your site was all about wood-working, then you might say, "When I get my next wood-working design and plan published, I'd like to make sure you know about it. Make sure you add yourself to my mailing list." Somebody who is interested in wood-working might add themselves to your newsletter or list. Now you have them captured. When you do have a new wood-working plan, you can let them know and put a buy now button below the description of the plan. They'll come check it out and some will buy.

That is what having a topic is about. This is very important. That reader in the example added themselves to your list because of their interest in the same things you are. They weren't interested in your products yet, but they might be later. You have him on your list now. You have the opportunity to start sending emails out automatically about everything else that you have.

REVIEW

Let's review what we've said so far about directories. You only need a small number of them. You can probably do just fine with one. You are going to submit them manually so there is no need for some kind of spinner tool. Automatic article submitters can be an example of the wrong way to succeed at article marketing. Other webmasters will visit the directory, see your article and want to re-use it on their site or sites. That is what gets you these links. You are working to get as many links as you can.

Do this right. You do not have to cheat. Use white hat techniques and stay as far away as you can from all the tips and tricks and black hat funny stuff. If you want a long term business, do this right. Just like any business in town, you start doing little funny things because you think it is going to make you a little bit more money and eventually, you will have to start over. Yes, maybe you will make a little bit more in the very short term, but you may have to start your business over from scratch in a few months because nobody will do business with you anymore. This is a huge world. You might even get away with it for a while, but a bad reputation is almost impossible to fix. If you want a long term business you can feel proud of, keep things honest.

Self-syndication is publishing your article in your own blog. Learn how to interlink your blogs if you have more than one. Get link-happy, but do not overdo it. Think about links as you are writing your articles. If you see something that you've written about before, highlight it and put a link to the other page. It is a little more work, but it is really important. Link on your keyword phrases as much as you can. Careful though, you can get too crazy. Two to three links in a 400 to 500 word article is perfectly acceptable.

Social media, Facebook, Twitter, and LinkedIn also are great links. Use them. Link back to your site. They are not as valuable as some of the other kinds of links that we've been talking about, but they are links.

The articles I post on my blog are all original. Play it safe and if you must spin, spin it good. I would like to add that if the majority of your site is good original material and the few that you have had published for creating links are also self-syndicated on your site using the HTML code they give you with no modifications, you are probably going to be just fine. Just do not overdo it.

FINDING YOUR ARTICLES AND MORE ON DIRECT SYNDICATION

Direct syndication means by-passing article marketing directories altogether and finding somebody who you can write articles for. Let's say a webmaster visited an article marketing site looking for content and decided to use your article. You will be notified by the article marketing directory, but in addition, I like to set up alerts that tell me when my name appears somewhere on the Internet by using http://www.google.com/alerts. Google alerts will send notifications. When you receive them, do a little bit of research and find out who used your article.

Analytics can be so important. You can tell who is re-publishing your articles. After you find out who it is, visit their site, find a contact page, and write them a note. Visit their site and make a comment like, "Hey, I see you published my article, thank you. That is awesome. I really appreciate that. Do you want more?" Only do this if you visit the site and you realize this site has lots of traffic. This webmaster might a good person to do a JV (joint venture) with. Some sites allow guest blogging. Perhaps after talking or emailing them, you will be able to write specific content for them.

You will want to make friends and talk over the phone for a website with a lot of traffic. There are all sorts of ways to benefit from a relationship like this. They might hire you to write for them. They might post a banner in return for you posting one for them. The basic thing is to have them publish your article in their blog or website and maintain that link back to you. This is another example of direct syndication. Make sure it is worth your while.

Let's say you've published four articles the last few weeks. You've looked to see how your articles have fared and discover a few people have seen fit to syndicate (re-publish) your article. These are those links we've been talking about. Where do you find your articles? Who published them? Where do they appear? Whoever these potential partners may be, you need to know. Google analytics or Google alerts may tell you.

There are some WordPress plugins that you can put on your blog that are really good. You may not even have to use Google Analytics. "Oh my, all of a sudden I'm getting a hundred hits a day from somewhere. Who is using my article?" This is somebody you may want to contact. I have a number of alerts set on Google Alerts. (http://www.google.com/alerts) You enter a keyword phrase, or your name, your author name, your website name, or whatever you want. Google Alerts is not a plugin, it's a service provided free by Google to alert you to any use of any keyword phrase you enter.

Google Alerts is a necessary tool for article marketers. It also gives you an eye on thieves who may possible want to steal your articles. Stealing your article means someone who borrows your content and won't maintain the links that the article marketing directory use agreement requires. It means they are using your article without the link you want.

In direct syndication you are looking for a link back to you. The best partner provides you that link and maybe a lot more. When you write an article for someone else, you want that article to be some sort of a trade.

There may be some unique content opportunities in direct syndication. You can ask your potential partner. Even better, get them on the phone and talk. They should be able to give you some ideas. They have a better idea of what people on their sites are reading than you would just by looking around. The submission guidelines for a direct syndication deal like this are completely new guidelines. It is totally between the parties involved and entirely up to the two of you how you structure the agreement. There are some advantages to making up the rules as you go.

THIEVES, PEOPLE STEALING YOUR MATERIAL

If somebody is re-using your article (syndicating it) and they are not using it correctly, that is not right. You want to be notified that your article was used. You might be notified by email, or by searches, or by a Google alert. Now you know it was published somewhere. You can visit their site and take a look. Make sure they have a link to you and a link to the article marketing site as required. You might even right-click the page, click on view-source, find the link to you in the HTML source code, and make sure there is not a "no-follow" on the link. No-follow instructs the search engines to go no further. It pretty much makes your links useless. The idea is for search engines to find these links, follow them back to you as the source of the original content, the authority site on this subject. An unscrupulous webmaster may attempt to deny you of the benefit of this link. If the webmaster did it right and used the HTML code provided by the article marketing site, there should be no issues, but not all article marketing sites are alike.

I will say that if someone is not familiar with the submission guidelines, they may have left the links out because they were just naïve. Naive can be fixed. But if there is a no-follow on a link, it is probably put there on purpose. You might have a thief on your hands. It happens. One of the requirements of an article marketing directory site's submission guidelines is a link to you, the author. If it's not there, the perpetrator in direct violation of the article directory's terms of service. These articles, once published, become copyrighted material. It is an asset that belongs to you. It is not ok for someone to use it this way. How do you deal with it?

DEALING WITH THIEVES

There are sites you can contact and sites you cannot which provide you two approaches - the soft and the not-soft. And there are three outcomes. First, the abuser deletes the content. You better check it again in a few months. People are so sneaky. Second, you find the abuser adds back your link. That is what you wanted. Again, you might have to go check later. It could be they "just forgot". Either that or they are new at this. There are newbies out there that haven't got a clue what they are doing. This is more than likely the typical thing that happens. They did not read the terms and conditions and they did not read the guidelines. There seems to be all kinds of reasons. Lastly, you just might be able to turn them into a direct syndication partner, which could be even better. You might get them on the phone, and they may say something like, "Oh my, I am so sorry. I did not realize I forgot those links." Since you had to go through all the trouble to find them, call them, and educate them, you might as well take the opportunity to at least talk about how you might help each other.

How do you go about contacting people? It is tedious, but you have to do it if you want to keep people from stealing from you. Like with anything else, you have to consider the return. Do not go nuts, fixate on it for a month, and walk around with the little black cloud over your head. It is just not worth all that. Are you going to keep 100 percent of your articles from being syndicated without that link? I'd say - probably not. There is always going to be a little bit of thievery here and there. It is just one of those things. That being said, I've never had anything happen to me. These days, Google is making duplicate content darn near worthless. Things are getting better. The Wild West of Internet days with every shady practice being used are slowing down. Balance your time. Is it worth spending all your time chasing some fool that has a totally duplicated article on his site with no traffic value when you ought to be out marketing and making money?

How do you find the contact information? Well, this is so silly sometimes. The easiest thing is to just go look. On most websites trying to make money, you will usually find an email address, skype name, maybe even a name and phone number. Most sites have contact information. If you are trying to make money, you cannot hide very well. There is also http://www.whois.com. It is not always the best way, but you can get plenty of information. Just a side note; do not be one of these people who pay extra for their sites to be anonymous, then plaster your name and phone number all over your site. Why do they pay extra to keep their name private for the registry, when they make it so easy to find their name and phone number? If you still can't find them, take a look on Google for their domain name. It is more than likely mentioned on another site.

What about those anonymous thieves or the ones that do not respond to your kind inquiries? You spent your time, you cannot find the person, or they won't respond. At some point you will have to consider http://www.dmcanotice.com. It is a nuisance to take time to do this, but you can send a website take-down notice. These notices work. Please be cautious. You have been warned. Do your due diligence, especially if this is someone you know who is stealing something from you. You can cause more trouble by having them taken down than just letting it go. The DMCA (Digital Millennium Copyright Act) people will take the site down until the situation is resolved. They will take it down until you agree that the situation is resolved. Be absolutely sure of yourself.

I have a friend who had a website about all kinds of communications antennas. A friend that worked with him had a disagreement over the use of certain words. The name, the book, and everything else on the site belonged to my friend. He wrote it, he owned it, he was the author, and had always been the only author. A product name they had shared in the company that existed some ten years earlier caused the disagreement. His friend decides he wants to cause some trouble. He submits a DMCA notice to the hosting company where the antenna website is hosted, and my friend's website and business is shut down. It took him two weeks to get it resolved.

The result was that nothing had to be changed on his site, but it cost him sales, time, anguish, and a lot of embarrassment. Do not do this unless you are really sure.

Nonetheless, if you tried to contact the evil-doers and you tried to rehabilitate them, or if they called you up and told you to take a hike, do the notice right away.

The site http://www.whois.com will reveal who the hosting company is for any website on the Internet. Whois.com will tell you where the website was registered, and it will tell you where it is hosted. Take a look and find what is called the "name servers". Then you can follow that to the hosting company. There are a lot of different ways to find the hosting company, but for the most part, you will be able to find it on whois.com. All the information you need to complete a DMCA Notice is right there.

So, what can you do short of the DMCA Notice? First will be the contacting phase. Try this. Once you reach them, pretend it was a mistake to begin with. "Hi, I am just trying to contact you regarding something you have published on your website. It belongs to me. I am the author. I wonder if you realized that you were supposed to have certain links on these posts. It is part of the submission guidelines of the article marketing directory site where it was published. I did some investigating and it looks like those links are gone. If you would not mind, could you please restore them?" You could put a link to the article's terms of service, email it to them, and give them a chance. Give them the benefit of the doubt. More than likely, they are newbies and haven't got a clue what they are doing, and forgot or did not do it on purpose. You never know. Do not assume.

You might try to work in your favor. You could say, "I really love your website. You have some great content. I am a writer and one of the articles you chose for your site was mine. I am honored to meet you, tell me more about what you are doing out here on the Internet." Then work in something about getting the links restored while possibly working a direct syndication deal. Of course, this is only if you find it was just a mistake and they could use some help with what they are doing.

If you give them a chance and they still haven't fixed anything and you are tired and angry now, then it is time to consider the DMCA Notice. If you've sent four or five emails and there are no phone numbers and no way to contact them, maybe it is time. Just remember though, they could possibly be on vacation.

RECAP

Let's recap. Our goal is to maximize syndication. In other words, our goal is to get our article published and have other people re-publish it. Our goal is not to get our article published on as many article marketing directories as we can, because that does not really matter. We want to get our articles published in the biggest article marketing directories there are, and have as many people as we can syndicate them, use them in their sites, so that we get these one-way links back to us. The end result for us as the author is to become the authority site, the origination of all things related to our topic. If all roads (links) lead back to you, then you would become the authority on that topic. Select the best directory. Then, if you have more than one site to submit to, sequence them so they are accepted. Depending on which ones you are going to select, they are all going to have different rules. Sequence them for your best exposure. EzineArticles.com for example, wants an absolutely original, never before published article, so they may have to be first and so on.

We can syndicate ourselves, of course. Syndicating ourselves means that once it is published, now we are able to use it just like any other webmaster. Remember the cautions here. We also have to remember that publishing articles is just a small part of an overall traffic strategy. We will be self-publishing all the other types of articles that we need for our website. We still have to maintain the links and adhere to all the rules in the submission guidelines like anyone else. After we get a few things published, it is time to find out where it was published. We might just take an opportunity and go direct. Our intent is to have other people use our articles so that we get links back to our site. You are providing other webmasters the content they want in return for something you want, which are the links. In the process, they will be doing a little marketing for you.

ENDLESS CONTENT

The Internet is based upon words. All those graphics and everything else that you see on all the pages are wonderful, but those are for human consumption. They are not for search engine consumption. Search engines do not see any of that. What they see is the back side of your page. If you ever want to take a look at what a search engine sees, open your browser, go to http://google.com. Enter any keyword phrase and click the "Google Search" button. The first page will contain the top listings for that keyword phrase. The first site must be the one that is ranking very well. Choose the first site and click on it. When the website appears, use your mouse and right click anywhere on the page. Select "View Page Source". Take a look at the source code. Somewhere in there if you can find it will be title, description and keyword Meta tags. If you can't see these right away, use the "Edit" menu and select "Find". Type "meta" and press enter. That should take you to the general area of the HTML code page where these Meta tags can be found. It may take a few minutes to locate your first time. You can't break anything so don't worry. This is what a search engine sees. You may call it gobbledygook, but that is HTML code. It is a lot of words with instructions in-between to tell the browser (Internet Explorer, Firefox, and Safari) what to do and how to display the page.

Search engines can match up certain words and attempt to use very some complicated algorithms to determine if the site and keyword phrases match well enough. If they do not match very well, the search engines may consider the site in question a spam site. Maybe someday these search engines will be able to make heads or tails of the content and the ideas inside quick enough. Every few days, search engine web crawlers have to take a look at every page on the Internet and index it. They have to read every word, find all the patterns of words, follow the links, read the meta tags, compare it to other sites, and a myriad of other tasks before they decide where to index the site. They have to do all of this for each site in a split second.

The point of this discussion is that one of the things we are trying to do with our efforts is to give these search engines content to index. You have to know what they are looking for before you can understand what to write. You already understand what humans like, you are one of them. Now you know you need to satisfy both your readers and the search engines to be successful. You've racked your brain, you've hurt your head, you've studied and studied and you've finally come up with a topic. This is the topic you are going to live with and make money with. Where can you find an endless supply of content for your topic?

VISIT http://www.Internetsalesfunnel.com for a free video on how to choose a topic. Choosing a topic is one of the most important long term decisions you can make regarding your business.

We're going to talk about how you can get endless content for your website. I have to change your thinking and present the idea of topic bridging. We are trying to bring people to our website based on the main topic, but at the same time, sell our products. We want to build content bridges from the main topic to all sorts of other topics so it seems your site is all about just the main topic. We want everything to somehow be related to the main topic. You will have no problem accomplishing this when we're done.

Here's a simple example: Let's say you are an affiliate for an advertising system of some kind. You are a member of a website like *Prospect Geyser, Advertise Your Business Now*, or maybe *Internet Sales Funnel*. Your topic is weight-loss coffee and you sell specialty coffees designed to help you lose weight. But *Advertise Your Business Now* has absolutely nothing to do with weight-loss coffee. How do you bridge them? How do you put them all together so they are all related?

Try this. "Hi, I have written many articles about weight-loss coffee. It is my passion. I have many articles; I hope you've enjoyed them. One of the tools that I've been using to help me sell weight-loss coffee in my Internet business is this advertising site called *Advertise Your Business Now*. I created an ad and I've gained these great targeted leads. I highly recommend that if you have an Internet business that you take the time to become a member at *Advertise Your Business Now*. Please click here." When they click the link, the reader is taken to your affiliate page at *Advertise Your Business Now*. Do you see how I bridged over from coffee to an advertising site? We're going to be talking about to do that and take it to crazy heights. It is what I call Endless Content.

While we go through this exercise, I want you to think of your own topic. If you have chosen one already, try and apply the examples as we go. We're going to do some topic bridging and explore some endless content ideas. We're going to use dog training and weight-loss coffee as example throughout this exercise.

TOPIC BRIDGING

If the solution of too little traffic is always more content, how do you come up with enough content? A simple process to create endless article topics is called *Topic Bridging*. Topic bridging finds angles and connections from the main topic to any other topic. In the Internet marketing world, it means finding a connection to the keyword phrase that you want to grab some traffic from. Remember, writing articles starts with the keyword phrase first and a little research. Now you have that keyword phrase and you are trying to come up with the content of the article.

Articles should be between 250 and 500 words long. If you are writing a viral article for an article marketing directory website, you want them to be at least 400 words long. If you have a longer article, split it up. If you had one long article that becomes two, use two different keyword phrases that you can rank for, and possibly receive twice the traffic. Link these articles together. Choose your keyword phrase carefully. You are going to use that keyword phrase as the title, a couple of times in the body of the article, in the description, the tags, and the SEO.

Remember, there are three kinds of articles; product articles, informational articles, and viral articles. The product articles are the sales pages which lead to a payment button. The viral articles are special articles written to attract links back to our site so we're not expecting that much traffic from them. The informational articles are where we get our traffic. Informational articles are always written about your site's main topic.

What kind of traffic are we expecting from these three types of articles? Organic traffic that comes from direct searches from search engines is one thing we're expecting. The informational articles will bring us most of our organic traffic. The viral articles will bring us some amount of syndication traffic. This traffic will come from other websites that have re-published one of our articles. We should not expect much traffic from these, but there will be some trickle of traffic anyway. The product articles will get some traffic as well and be ultra-targeted. This traffic will probably mostly be people already looking specifically to buy the product. All of this traffic comes from content. If we need as much traffic as we can get, then we need as much content as we can get to attract that traffic. Each article we write is written using the methods described earlier so that each article is written to command a particular keyword phrase. It does not hurt to have too much content.

OTHER TRAFFIC METHODS

There are lots of other ways to get traffic to your website besides writing articles. You might purchase traffic through solo ads. You can create traffic through pay per click ads from Google Ad Words or Bing Ads. You can use Safelists, Traffic Exchanges, and Ad Rotators. These are all paid traffic methods. This book concentrates on the free stuff.

All traffic helps create page ranking. Links also help create page ranking. The better the page ranking, the more traffic search engines direct your way. The more traffic your site receives, the more keyword phrases your site commands, the more original content your site contains, the more links lead to your content, the more your site becomes the authority on your topic. The more authority you command, the more traffic the search engines send your way. That is how all this works. The best kind of traffic is from content. That is the free stuff created through keyword attraction by the articles we write.

Let's describe what they call long-tailed attractors. A long-tailed attractor is just a search term, a keyword phrase that has more than one word in it. The more words in a keyword phrase, the longer the tail attractor. As time goes on and the Internet collects more and more content, you may realize that you have to type in five or six words to find anything on the Internet. If you think back a few years ago, when the Internet was virtually empty in a lot of subjects, you could type one or two words in a search and you would find what you needed quickly. That just does not work anymore. Sometimes you have to type an entire question to get close to the answer you were looking for. The result is that keyword phrases have become longer and longer in an amazingly short few years. We're going to start by trying to find a keyword phrase that has a fair amount of traffic, but as little competition as possible. Keep this in mind as we search for subjects to write about within our topic.

The problems of not having enough traffic can be solved by more content. Make sure this concept gets inside your brain. One of the ways to create an endless supply of content is this concept of topic bridging. Topic bridging is breaking out of your topic and finding ways to relate your main topic to almost anything. How does one figure that out when most of us cannot think of more than 250 words on our entire topic? Most of us seem to be completely brain dead after that. You have to break out of your topic. You have to make some bridges. You have to make all of your topics your topic. Viral articles are the exception. Viral articles do not really even have to be related to your topic. You can go viral no matter how offbeat your product or market is, but everything else must be related back to your topic. Are you confused yet? The solution to the problem of topics and endless content is a kind of trivia game. Hopefully this will put this in perspective for you.

The game is called the *Kevin Bacon Game* or the *Six Degrees of Kevin Bacon* after the phrase: *six degrees of separation*. It is an actual game you can find at http://www.thekevinbacongame.com. Kevin Bacon once claimed that he had worked with everyone in Hollywood and this game tests his claim. The game determines the degree of separation between any two actors - alive or dead - between Kevin Bacon and the actor chosen. It is very hard to obtain a score higher than 6. It is also very rare to find actors that aren't connected at all. An example would be Elvis Presley who is in "*Change of Habit*" with Edward Asner, while Edward Asner was in "*JFK*" with Kevin Bacon. Asner and Bacon have no direct relationship whatsoever, but because Elvis Presley was in a movie with Edward and Edward was in a movie with Kevin, they are related and have a distance number. The Asner-Bacon distance in this case is two.

Connecting topics together on your website is the same thing. Every topic is connected with everything else in some way, shape, or form. The point is: *do not write on topic, write on connections.* The connections are what are called bridges. Using this kind of topic bridging, you can have unlimited topics. Each individual bridge is called a *topic pairing*.

TOPIC PAIRING

Let's explore some topic pairing examples. Let's take dog training and weight-loss coffee to try this out. Our first pairing in dog training is dogs and law. Let's explore this pair a little further. What are some laws that have anything to do with a dog? Barking can be a public nuisance. How about cleaning up while you are on a walk? Different cities have different laws for dogs and they vary all over the world. There are also dog biting ordinances. There is a situation happening here in my home town. The city is trying to make the person that owns the house - not the renter - responsible for the renter's dog. That means that at some point or another, if you own a dog, nobody is ever going to rent a house to you. There are very current laws like this example and there are very old laws which do not even apply anymore. What kinds of things are going on in your town? What about insurance? What about special status for certain kinds of dogs like police dogs and Seeing Eye dogs?

What about our other example? This one I chose from one of our focus groups as one of the stranger ones. Let's take weight-loss coffee and law. What kind of laws surrounds weight-loss coffee? The moment you claim its weight-loss, it could affect your health. You better have some kind of proof to back it up.

How did these kinds of laws come into being? How much actual proof do you need? You could write about all the laws where there have been claims made about weight-loss which really did not work - or maybe they did not tell the whole truth. If you are trying to sell weight-loss coffee, talk about why your particular kind of coffee is valid and not a scam. You may actually bring a lot of traffic in just because people are looking on the Internet to see if weight-loss coffee itself is a scam. That can be a great keyword phrase even though there is no scam at all. People are always checking before they buy. Capitalize on that fact. You will be able to say, *"Everybody's complaining about this weight-loss scam. It is not true. Here are the facts."* You have the opportunity to turn people around. You will catch both the positive and negative traffic.

What about other laws that might affect weight-loss products in general? It seems to me, you can go crazy with this subject. But let's keep our focus on coffee. What about laws having to do with coffee? How is it produced? Certain countries have a lot of rules on coffee production. For example, if you want to be able to say, *"Made in Brazil"*, the coffee must meet certain standards. It can be sold locally to anybody, but if it is going to be exported out of the country and say *"Product of Brazil,"* there are more requirements. What about getting it out of the country? What about customs? What kind of fees are assessed, how is it shipped, how is it packaged, and on and on? People are searching on the Internet for information like this.

Let's say a small coffee shop is considering importing coffee to save a little money. This is a subject they need to investigate. It works with your topic. They visit your site, find out about your weight-loss coffee and say, "Hmmm, I do not have any weight-loss coffee in my shop. That might sell well. Maybe I need to buy some. How can I contact this guy? Ah, here's a phone number and an email". Click.

What about cleaning up? How can cleaning up be related to weight-loss coffee? Are there any rules about coffee grinds and coffee waste? Is weight-loss coffee different than regular coffee? Do the grinds have to be treated any differently after the coffee is made? What makes it different from regular coffee? You can write articles about all of this. Have there been any reported illnesses? If you are a coffee producer or if you are importing coffee, is there any liability to be aware of, any special kind of insurance that you've got to have in order to import, produce, brew, roast, etc.? If you just have a coffee house and you are serving weight-loss coffee, or selling weight-loss coffee in packages, is there any concern one way or the other on having some kind of insurance in case somebody gets a bad batch? Once you start exploring the pairing, the content possibilities just go on and on and on.

What about dog professions? On the dog side, we have police dogs, guard dogs, companion dogs, bomb and drug sniffing dogs, dogs that make movies and TV shows, and everything else. If dogs were your thing, it's endless. You can do reviews on different dog shows and anything else related to dogs. You have TV shows like the *Dog Whisperer* and *Pit Bulls and Parolees.* How and where are these kinds of dogs bred? Are there specific requirements for different kinds of dogs? How are they bred this way? How are they trained? It is a huge subject. People spend their entire life learning how to train dogs.

Let's talk about who trains them. What about "a day in the life of a working dog"? What kind of life does a regular working dog have? Does a police dog have a different kind of life than a guard dog? Do more research. Find sites that have written articles about these subjects and "cure them". Re-write them and make them more current. It's called *content curation.* Let's say you found something about how they were training dogs ten years ago in Brazil. Curate the article. *"This is what they were doing in Brazil ten years ago and this is what they are doing now".* When do dogs retire? What is the working life of a dog and when do they end up in the old dog's home? Do different kinds of dogs retire earlier? I know sometimes police dogs are only good for a few years, but some people keep a seeing-eye dog the entire dog's life.

What about professions related to weight-loss coffee? There might be a lot of people wondering how to market coffee on the Internet. You already know how. (You read this book). You could be the expert on marketing weight-loss coffee. Other professions related to weight-loss coffee might be growers, harvesters, and processors. Somebody's has to grow it. Somebody has to harvest it and get it to a processor. Somebody has to process it. How does it become weight-loss coffee? There has to be some sort of a laboratory process. It usually is decaffeinated with extra health benefits. How did they get the caffeine out? If this is your topic, these are the things you would want to write about.

What is decaffeinated coffee exactly? Why is it considered a weight-loss product? What kind of companies are they? Did they add or take out ingredients? Where do those ingredients come from? Who figured all that out? As far as professions go, you've got everything from the guy who picked the original bean, wherever they got the bean, the guy who brought it to market, the guy who sold it to an exporter, the guy who exported it, and the guy who distributes it in your country. You have all of the people in the professions that modify the product from the original bean to what it is now. Then you have distribution. There are a lot of people involved if you really think about what goes into a product.

You can find a lot of information on the Internet. Tear it apart, comment on it, research it, put it all together and make it your own. Take one page and turn it into six or seven. We're demonstrating endless content and we're thinking about all of the different ways that you can bridge into other topics and make all kinds of pairings.

What about the history of dogs. There are many different breeds of dogs. Every dog has to be trained, but training a Chihuahua is a lot different than training a Saint Bernard. I'm sure there are very different ways that you have to go about it. How about discussing when dogs were first domesticated? We're talking a very, very long time ago. Different countries domesticated their animals at different times. You could write about all of these subjects. What were dogs used for over time? What were they used for 3,000 years ago? You can talk about all the different uses that they have had since the beginning of time. We talked about all the different professions, but we actually haven't talked about all of the other uses a dog can have. What were the original uses for each breed?

The oldest recognizable dog breeds are the Greyhounds and the Mastiff dogs. In ancient Egypt and western Asia, images were found of dogs that are likely descended from a few thousand B.C. Mastiffs were used in Roman arenas to fight and Greyhounds were used mainly for their speed in hunting prey. The heavier Mastiff dogs were used in war and as guard dogs. There were dogs found embalmed in ancient Egypt. Archaeologists found small dogs, which served as a burial gift to the dead. These small dogs have much of today's Dachshund and Teckel in them. Some dog breeds are very old, but most are created in the last few centuries. What was the original use for each one of these breeds? There is a lot of history and a lot to write about.

Now, if we are talking weight-loss coffee, you have a very specific product that is made from a Panama Bouquet Coffee Bean. Why and who chose that particular bean? Is there any way to find out? You can compare it to different kinds of other types of beans. Then write about the history of coffee. Why and when did humans start drinking coffee? Who figured out that you could toast a bean and make coffee out of it? Do different countries make coffee differently? How did it spread across the world?

I remember reading that coffee made it to England through an explorer in a ship. The Queen tried it and she liked it. She liked it so much; it quickly ended up the number-one morning drink in the castle. What is the number one coffee bean in the world? Compare it to other coffee beans, and so on. What are the uses of coffee throughout time? You can talk about how coffee has been used throughout the years, and we are talking thousands of years. How did we start using it for a weight-loss product? Lots of people wake up every day and they drink coffee first thing. I drink a pot a day myself. (I'm not losing much weight with the stuff I drink) What were the original uses for coffee? Did it ever have any other use? I'm sure there is a lot of information on many other weight-loss products. Why would coffee be a good weight-loss product? You could write a number of articles on that particular question.

AM I JUMPING AROUND?

If it seems like I am jumping around, you would be right. We are taking different pairings and using the topics of dog training and weight-loss coffee as examples, remember? When you apply your own topic to the pairings, I hope this exercise will give you plenty of ideas on how to pair-up your topic and create your own endless content.

What about training animals other than dogs? There are mules, horses, and cats and many other animals that could be trained. What about cats? You can talk about why it is impossible to train a cat to be a seeing-eye cat. That might be a funny article. An article illustrated like that just might be humorous enough to go viral.

Try this. Get your cat and put a leash on it. Put a little sweater on your cat that says "*Seeing Eye Cat*". Have your cat walking around leading you into walls. Do a little video and put it on YouTube. That is probably politically incorrect, but it would be pretty funny. A video like that would go viral because that is just hilarious. Maybe try filming a person posing as a cat herder trying to herd fifteen or twenty cats with a toy whip or something. That is one way to get your links. What about dogs and cats together?

Let's apply this to weight-loss coffee. I remember in my history book reading about how insurance on shipping from London to the colonies in America started. Coffee houses were popular in London. One coffee house was named *Lloyd's of London.* Insurers and shippers would use the private rooms at Lloyd's to conduct the business of insuring ships that were carrying products across the ocean. The history of coffee, coffee houses, production, countries, everything revolving around coffee will keep you busy writing for years.

How about the relationship between dogs and other animals? For example, dogs and horses. What about dogs and cows? What about the differences between dogs and wolves? If wolves were domesticated to become dogs, why cannot we domesticate wolves? There is a lot you could write about.

Let's also discuss coffee. Since you cannot train coffee, we could write about the relationship between coffee and other products. Why not write about weight-loss coffee combined with exercise? Why not write about weight-loss coffee combined with some other weight-loss product? Has there been any study or does anyone have any opinion about weight-loss coffee combined with other types of weight-loss products? Are there some relationships that are good or some that may be harmful to you if you try to do too much? What about the relationship between coffee beans and tea? Someone said *"Coffee gives me energy to train my dog"*. That is funny.

What about wild coffee? We are talking about weight-loss coffee so it won't be wild, but what about the original product? Coffee is a shrub or tree. What does a coffee tree look like? How many varieties of coffee are there? What is the difference between them? Can all of them be made into coffee for human consumption? How is it grown? How do you water it? Who waters it? Where is it grown specifically in the world? Did the wild coffee bean actually grow wild?

This weight-loss coffee bean we are using as an example comes from Panama. Panama is a very tropical country. Write about being on the equator. Is this bean native to Panama? How did coffee get to Panama in the first place? How did it all start? What are the best conditions for coffee to grow? If you talk to somebody in Brazil, they'd probably argue with you if you said Panama grows the best coffee bean. Or maybe Colombia grows a better bean.

Is there an impact on humans? You could talk about the impact of coffee on humans throughout history and you could talk about the impact of weight-loss coffee on humans. What has been the impact on yourself, on your friends, on the people that have bought and used the product? Before and after photos would add emphasis.

Let's get back to dogs and talk about wild dogs. There are coyotes and wolves. There are wild dogs in Australia called dingoes and there are wild dogs in Australia called wild dogs. Are today's coyotes related to wolves? Can you train one? What is the history of each kind of wild dog and where are they now? How and why do they hunt? Which dogs are the best to train as hunters? We train them to swim out to a duck after you shoot it and put it in its mouth without eating it. That is amazing.

You could also write about the impact wild dogs have had on livestock and humans. We could write about stray dogs. How many stray dogs are there? Is the number growing? Is it getting smaller? Are stray dogs a problem when they become pets? Can you train them? You can talk about feral versus stray dogs and feral cats and bringing them back into our world. It is sometimes very problematic. What are those problems and how are they solved? People sure do love dogs.

I do not believe I've ever heard of stray coffee – unless it was growing wild where it wasn't wanted. Let's write about the number of people that are drinking weight-loss coffee as compared to regular coffee. People love their coffee. How many people drink weight-loss coffee? Is this movement growing? Are there weight-loss coffee groups? Is there only one kind of weight-loss coffee out there? Are there any other stray products that claim to be weight-loss coffee products? Are they as good or are they not as good? Do they have the same vitamins, benefits, and taste? If you drink too much of it, can it hurt you? These are all questions your readers will want to know before they buy from you.

What if you just think that you can drink decaffeinated coffee and take vitamins to lose weight? Maybe you could drink *Maxwell House* decaffeinated coffee and take vitamins and get the same effect. That would be a stray version of it, would not it? There are many different angles that you could explore. Whew! Are you getting the idea yet? There is just an endless amount of content when you take a few moments to brainstorm and think about it.

We haven't even touched on theories. What are the theories that are involved in dog training? There definitely are a lot of different theories. There is everything from a dog-whisperer to a buggy whip. Both probably work although I'd rather not have a disgruntled, whipped, and beaten dog. What of the after-effects? Is one method better than another? How have those theories changed over the years? This could be a large subject.

When it comes to coffee, how did this new weight-loss thing come about? How are they modifying coffee to be able to use it as a weight-loss product? What are the theories involved and why is it a good way to go?

What about tools and techniques? When it comes to dog training, there are a lot of different tools and techniques. Theories are more of an overall look from above. Techniques are exactly how to actually, physically do the training. When you talk coffee, we can discuss why and how you should cook it or brew it. Think about all the different ways of making the coffee. Is it instant coffee or is it beans that you grind? Can you use a French press? Is it better? Is it worse? Are there different benefits that you get out of each one of those methods? What is the history of how tools, techniques and theories came about and how they changed over time? You could cover the entire history of coffee. I know the main topic in this example is weight-loss coffee, but people are interested in coffee in general and how it is been transformed into a weight-loss product.

Please do not forget that this part of the book is about topic bridging. The idea is to bring in traffic to your website through organic searches. People who are asking questions they have about the coffee or dogs in our examples will hopefully find you in a search and visit your site. The site needs to answer their questions and raise more questions. People come to visit your site because they are interested in coffee or dogs. Be happy to answer any question for them and always have a call to action.

Now we go to famous trainers. You've all heard of Cesar Millan, the Dog Whisperer. Over the centuries, all the different breeds had a group or several groups that created a particular breed for a particular purpose. There are hundreds of breeds. That means there are hundreds of people who were famous in dog training. On the coffee side, who are the people involved? Who are the players? In this kind of a product, you might talk about the successful salespeople who are doing well selling it. What are they doing that made them successful? This is a special weight-loss coffee so there has to be some engineers, some doctors, and others who made this revolutionary product possible.

What is the point of all of this? I just covered at least thirty three different article titles. How far can you go with this? Is your topic so strange that you cannot do this? It is called brainstorming, isn't it? I'm hoping that having gone through this exercise with you that I opened up an absolutely endless number of things that you can write about. In fact, there were so many possible articles that some of the subjects opened even more huge cans of possibilities. If you open the can up, you can find thousands of articles.

CONTENT IS GREAT, BUT HOW DO YOU MAKE MONEY AT IT?

Let's talk about how you monetize your topic. It is fine to say I like dogs and I write articles about dogs, but there has to be a reason that you are going to do all the work required to create all these articles. The answer is to make a living doing something you love. To make a living on the Internet, you have to sell something. If your topic is about dogs, and you are talking about dogs, what would you sell? Maybe you would sell cool and silly dog clothes for different events that you or someone in your family makes. Maybe you don't sell them at all. Maybe you just sell the patterns and do how-to videos. Maybe you sell all kinds of dog clothes from a number of different sources drop shipped to your clients. Maybe you even find someone who can do special order custom designs. Whatever it is, it should be something more unique or harder to find. On the other hand, don't sell what someone can get at Walmart either. There are a million things that Walmart does not carry and there are plenty of items to sell that are unique to your part of your country that can't be found anywhere else. Don't worry about competition too much. You are going to learn how to do a better job than the next guy online. Dog clothes may sound silly, but it is actually big business. Have you ever tried to find some clothes around your town for your dog, even just a sweater for a short haired dog? It is not that easy. I have to go online. If you have to go online to find something you need because the items are hard to find anywhere in town, you have found something to sell. There are lots of ideas, but the articles bring the traffic, the products make you money. You get the idea.

The type of business or products you sell should be about what you like to do. It is nice that someone gives you a product to sell, but try and make this about what you want. That is what this book is about. It is not about confining you to whatever everybody else is selling on the Internet. You do not have to do that. A long term business will be something you have ultimate control over. Find more than one item, many is better. Have enough items that one or two becoming unavailable will not affect you.

Whether you make the dog clothes yourself or you have agreements with other dog clothes manufacturers that you want to sell on the Internet, you are going to be better at selling on the Internet than everybody else because you know my secret. This brings up a question.

WHO IS YOUR COMPETITION?

You may think there is a lot of competition out there, but there just isn't as much as you think. It depends on many factors. Who do you think your competition is? **Doc Stone Tip:** Your competition is the other guy who has figured out how to do the search engine optimization for his pages a little better than you. Maybe he is on page one of a Google search and you are only on page two. They get the business. You do not. Of course there may be a huge store downtown. You do not want to compete with it if you can avoid it. A small store downtown is not always competition for you. The small retailer with no real internet presence may even become a partner. They may have items you can buy together for the sake of buying power. They may have items you can sell online for them for a margin of profit. You should be worried about the people on the Internet who are using the same keyword phrases as you. Since you have no store-front, the competition is all online. That means your competition revolves around keyword phrases and search engines. Just remember that if you use different keyword phrases thinking obliquely like we have discussed already, you can get yourself off into another area where you do not have much competition at all.

WHAT IF I HAVE A WEIRD TOPIC?

So maybe you think your topic is so strange that you are not going to be able to "Topic Bridge" your way through it? Is there anything stranger than Buddhist Mandalas? Do you know what a Buddhist Mandala is? They are prayer creations that are made out of colored sand, or other similar materials. If you bump them, they are gone. Mandalas are usually round, and they have very intricate patterns. Believe it or not, several people have websites about Buddhist Mandalas. The point is - if they can make money from a website so unique and different, you can too.

Choosing a Topic

Here is a summary the process. You chose your topic. What is it? What will you start with? We chose two topics as examples. We chose dog training and weight-loss coffee. Then we explored a number of bridge topics. The choice of a bridge topic depends on the purpose of the content. This is what we are going to be talking about next. I touched on this earlier. There are three types of articles; product articles, informational articles, and viral articles. We are going to pick a bridge topic. What is your purpose? Is your purpose to go viral? Is your purpose a product article which is closely related to making a sale on a product you carry? Or is the article just going to be informational?

Once you have chosen our topic, you need to find keyword phrases that will be the title of the article. Use a browser and do a little research on keyword phrases. Find a keyword phrase that seems like it has little competition. You might have to add a few extra words in the word count of the phrase to find something with less competition. You will pick up more traffic with a little bit of research. We will be talking about this more later. You want to pick up the traffic available for that keyword phrase. The traffic has to go somewhere. You want that somewhere to be your site.

On-site content is closely related to what it is we are selling and what we have already published in our own blog. Off-site content is articles we have published in an article marketing directory site like viral articles. In a viral article, the Bacon distance can be eight to ten Kevin Bacons away, we are just bridging out as far as we can. This article does not go on our blog anyway, it is published on the article marketing directory site. Its purpose is to generate links back to us. We need both traffic and links in order to have our site rank properly. The greater Bacon distance that a viral article being published allows creates more opportunity because now we do not need to stay within our topic that much in order to come up with something viral.

A viral article can create a lot more opportunity and popularity, but getting it to go viral is not an easy thing. It takes imagination and work. You really have to think about it. I'm a musician. Many times, deep in the darkest part of the night, I find a melody stuck in my head and it wakes me up. I write it down immediately, even if it is three o'clock in the morning. Everybody's asleep, I have to be quiet. I cannot even see where I'm going. I creep into my office, get my camera going and turn on my recorder which is a double click away. I whisper the melody and the words that I had in my head. Then I can go back to sleep. If I don't do this, I will be up for the next couple of hours trying not to forget the melody. If I fall back to sleep, I will forget it. It is gone. Sometimes you have to grab ideas when they come. It does not help to say, "Oh, I had a wonderful idea last night, but I cannot remember what it was."

TOPIC TAXONOMY

Your topic selection for product articles should have your core product service or offer. I want to discuss what is called topic taxonomy. Topic taxonomy is basically a way to group articles together. As you are writing your articles, it is good practice to group them together. That helps in linking articles together. Remember, I said that when writing the article, use the keyword phrase at least twice in the body of the article. One should be **bolded**; one should be linked to another page. One reason to group articles together, is to easily have another page to link to within your blog. Here's another. As you do your research on keyword phrases, its good practice to have at least twelve to fifteen keyword phrases that you will use for your WordPress "tags" and the SEO plugin keyword phrases section. That is your grouping and your keyword article block. Each time you choose a topic and find twelve to fifteen phrases, write an article for each phrase, and link them together. There is more power in using related keyword phrases in a grouping like this. If you think this way, you are thinking topic taxonomy.

The easiest way to link articles together is to use the "chain link" icon in your editor when you write your articles. Your topic taxonomy block of twelve to fifteen articles, each one using one of the keyword phrases as its title, will be the articles we want to link together. Let's say you are writing your fourth article for this block. Use one of other three keyword phrases used in the titles of the other three articles you wrote creatively in this new article. The topics are going to be closely related so this should not be difficult. Highlight the keyword phrase you used with your mouse and press the chain link icon. Then type in the URL of the page that uses this keyword phrase in its title in the space provided and save it. Don't overdo your links. One or two per page should be sufficient. If you did some research on the keyword phrase, you will know what your competition is doing with their keyword phrases and why they are ranking on page one. We want to do one more thing than they did. We're going to discuss this philosophy in much more detail later.

COMMON BRIDGING PATTERNS

The most common bridging patterns are persons, places, things, activities, and time. Remember those five patterns. You will have plenty of areas and places to go with whatever your topic. More content equals more traffic, and if you can bridge, you can reach an endless supply of topics. Use bridges for both on-site and off-site content. By on site, I mean on your own blog, by off-site, I mean on article marketing sites.

MORE ON PRODUCT ARTICLES

I have said before that there are three types of articles needed for our blog. This is one of the most critical concepts to understanding how to structure your blog, what needs to go on the blog, what items go elsewhere, and what those items are. Product articles talk about what each product is and what each product does. These articles usually lead to a payment button somewhere where prospective clients can give you their money. These articles are closely related to sales conversions. The article should catalogue features and benefits of the product but it should be more than just a catalog page. After a prospective client has researched their problem and this product you sell seems to be the one to fix it, the article's job specifically is to lead the reader to, "I've got to have this, where do I click?" It is a very specific article that gives the reader the assurance that this product solves their problem. You have them at the door to buy, this is your closing. This is where you take their order. There should be at least two articles like this for every product you carry. If a product is selling well, you may want to have many articles about this product, each of them using every related keyword phrase you can find. Let's say you love watching TV. You love it so much that you found some little gadget that enables you to watch TV in every room in the house and outside in the yard as well. You had a lot of trouble finding it, but you persevered. You called the manufacturer and asked if you could market their product. They happen to have to reseller program and you find you can make a decent thirty percent margin after costs. The manufacturer has a minimum of five units for each purchase. I'm making this entire scenario up, but you would be surprised how easy it is to become a reseller. You make twenty dollars after expenses on every one you sell. For some reason, people cannot find it at the local store. It is only sold online and it's hard to find online if you don't know what to ask for.

This is a great example of an opportunity. People can not only find it out on your website because you are a better marketer than everybody else, they can also get a short recorded tutorial about how to hook it up from an expert and lots of other add-ons from your site. They click the payment button and you get an email saying you received an order. If you have a drop-ship agreement with the manufacturer, you call them and they ship one for you to wherever you want and bill you. If you have to buy five and have them shipped to you, you buy five, wait for them to arrive, ship one to your client and you have four left. If you sell 100 in a month, you will make $2000 a month in income.

That is just one of the items you found to sell. As you continue growing your business and your niche, you find more unique items for people's TVs. Each one of those items would have at least two articles in your blog. Each one of these pages details the features and benefits of each item. Make sure there is at least one picture of the item. It could have a video of how the item works. If you can get a few testimonials from happy clients, add those too. Detail what a client receives in their purchase exactly. Make sure the product page details the item costs, shipping, and handling. Don't forget the payment button.

MORE ON INFORMATIONAL ARTICLES

Informational articles are written on topic. These are what bring traffic to your site. They always lead to a product page. Let's use our example; your topic is TV - daytime TV specifically. Let's say you are writing articles about a soap opera. The informational articles will be about what is happening on the shows, articles about the players on screen and off screen, the people who make them, how and where they are made, and everything you can think of. These articles always have a call to action. One of the things you might at the end of an article is "By the way, I like to watch my soap opera in every place in my house, even when I'm watering my plants. I never want to miss a second of programming. I found this awesome way of piping the video everywhere and I only own one receiver from my TV provider. Click here for more information".

By the way, as I was researching this book, I realized that online TV is huge. There is so much to know about where to watch your shows online, how to stream them to different devices, and the works. There are affiliate programs on most of these online sites that you may be able to take advantage of. My point in using TV as an example is that even if you are not getting off your couch anytime soon, there are still opportunities out there for you to make your hobby pay for itself.

Informational articles should always start with the keyword phrase you want to rank for. You need to decide how you are going to bridge to your topic and products. Think about every little problem that your product could possibly ever solve. As the reader arrives to discover that someone understands what they are going through and actually has a solution, they are happy to discover a link that brings them to the very item that will make their life better.

MORE ON VIRAL ARTICLES

Viral articles are designed to create one-way links back to your site. The Bacon distance does not have to be close at all. A relationship to your topic is desirable, but not necessary. These articles are useful purely for links back to your site. You will always publish these on an article marketing site of some kind, preferably the biggest ones out there. I should say that once in a while, you may publish a really good informational article, but for the most part, only viral articles will be published. Since most article marketing sites require an absolutely original, never before published article, you will have to submit it to the article marketing site first and wait until it gets published.

Do not write viral articles in your blog. Use an offline editor. Other webmasters may choose to syndicate (re-publish) your article. You want to have your articles syndicated as often as possible with links from sites that are unrelated to yours. It's really helpful when the sites that re-publish your article are sites that get a large amount of traffic. The main thing with a viral article is that the subject needs to be a topic that other people want to read and share. They can be funny, sad, of human interest, timely, newsy, about current events, or almost anything. The more it is shared, the more viral it gets. Don't worry about getting 500 links with every article; just get as many as you can.

AN ARTICLE TYPE I DIDN'T MENTION

There is one more kind of article not worth mentioning. These articles are all the articles that we shouldn't use. They are the poor quality articles you may have written or hired someone to write and they just weren't up to your standards. You might have written an article for a particular keyword because it looked like there was some traffic there, but when you're done with the article, you felt it wasn't very good. I would suggest you fix them or do not use them. Fix it so that it becomes one of the other kinds of articles. Have some pride in what you are doing and realize that the search engines won't know it is a poor quality article, but your readers will. In addition, a webmaster will decide if they want to re-publish it. They won't re-publish a poorly written article. If you don't fix them, just forget them.

MUCH MORE ON PRODUCT ARTICLES

Let's get more detailed. Let's start with product articles. Again, these are primarily going to be posted on your blog. They are not for syndication. They have the highest quality content, at least for you, because it is essentially the features and benefits of items you can sell. They have the most direct influence on conversions and sales because they lead directly to a payment button. They should involve the reader emotionally. What will life be like after I own this item? They should motivate the reader to want, even need to take advantage of your offer and want to become an owner of your product or service. It is the narrowest range of topics because the article is specifically about the product that you have that you sell. You should have at least two or more for each product you have. Only write more on a particular item because it is selling well.

What kind of things would you write about? Let's start with features, advantages, and benefits. These are much more than just a catalog page. These pages will lead directly to a payment button. You can also write articles that become product comparisons. I call them selectors. Product comparisons can be only comparing products you carry or you can compare your products to the competition. In the article, highlight the top five or ten features of each and compare them. These need to be similar products that do the same thing or provide the same kind of service. If you carry all the five types of products yourself, it really does not matter which product they choose. You make a sale either way. It is a lot easier for a prospective client to make a decision when you've done all the comparison shopping for them. If you say "top five" and you are referring to a generic top five, you need to have a reasonable knowledge of what the top five might be. Do the research. You could also say "Your Top Five" if you wanted to and be perfectly right in saying so.

Remember, this book is about gaining *Web Authority*. You will become an expert and an authority on your topic over time. You are saying that these products are the top five that you think they are. You do not really care which one they take as long as they choose one that works well for them and they are ultimately satisfied. A word of caution about this; if there are another five products that are similar and well known and you leave them out of your comparison, your readers will know and not trust you. You may not be able to procure an agreement to sell those products, but do not leave them out of your comparison. There will always be a reason why the product you have should be considered. It may be the price or the overall value as compared to a better, more expensive product, but there will always be a reason.

YOU SHOULD HAVE A NICHE.

You have created a niche. You have a specialty and an area of expertise. People do not achieve recognition and popularity by being okay at something. No average basketball player ever made the NBA, let alone became famous. Your goal is to find a niche and own it with an excellent understanding of your content and market by providing great material that people cannot get elsewhere. It is not as hard as you think, but it does take time. That is one of the things I teach.

Watch free webinar replays about choosing a topic and monetizing it called "Finding your Niche" If you would like to join our community and find out about live webinars and have the kind of training and resources I'm discussing in this book, get signed up for notifications at http://www.Internetsalesfunnel.com

When we talk about keywords and long tail searches and SEO, everybody gets confused. What I'm referring to is the words that you type in on Google or some other search engine. A few years ago, you could type in "blanket" and you would find thirty or forty sites to buy a blanket. You chose one and visited the site. If you type just one word like "blanket' in today, you will get a million choices. It is impossible to find anything. You end up typing more words, don't you? Today, you have to type more and more words in order to find what you are looking for. The goal in your search is to narrow the choices back down to that thirty or forty. You really are trying to find a place to buy a blanket preferably somewhere near your home.

This is all good news for new marketers. The playing field is always changing. The big companies in some cases haven't updated their sites in a while. They are still trying to attract visits using two or three keywords in a phrase. The reality is a lot of large companies are resorting to paid advertising these days thinking that the good old search engines aren't working anymore. They are right. These companies cannot do what they used to do and have a successful ad campaign. On top of that, they aren't trying to follow what I'm teaching in this book either. The reality is that they aren't trying to rank for keyword phrases that are much longer. That allows small time marketers like us to pick up traffic from internet surfers who are having to type in these longer phrases. Surfers have to type as many as seven to nine words in a phrase to find what they are looking for, but few are doing the SEO work for those longer phrases. Most big companies do not bother. They would rather spend more money on Google Ads. Google Ads work very well, but they can be incredibly expensive if you are not extremely careful. I've seen too many companies pay big money for two-word keyword phrases. You just cannot find what you are looking for with just two words. I'm not writing this book to show you how to spend money on ads that aren't working and cost lots of money. I'm telling you the secret to attracting free traffic from the good old search engines like we used to when Google and Yahoo were born. A lot of people think that cannot be done anymore. I disagree wholeheartedly. I do it all the time and can prove its effectiveness.

Because keyword phrase length has increased, there are more keyword phrases to rank for. This is good news for us; it means the little guys can actually compete. Remember, I spoke of who your competition really is with whatever product you have. It is not the store downtown that just might have the same item you carry for the same price. You are working online. Forget them. There is a great big world out there. Your competition is the person with the website that is doing a better job with their SEO work than you are. On the Internet, that is your next door neighbor. Find out what they are doing and do it better. Product articles are very specific to your products and usually the keyword phrases have much less competition hence the ranking benefits for your pages are a lot easier to realize.

ARTICLE MASS

Article mass is important. What I mean is that over time you will have more and more articles. Each time you write an article, it will be keyed to a particular keyword phrase. The phrases should be all related especially to each bridge topic you make from your main topic. Because you will have a lot of articles, the overall site mass helps the shorter tail searches rank higher than they would on their own. The more articles you have and the more keywords phrases which link to your site, the better the ranking. There are significant traffic benefits. These product articles will get natural links from the search engines over time. These types of articles also make good pages for social marketing and for comparisons.

MUCH MORE ON INFORMATIONAL ARTICLES

Informational articles can sometimes be published and syndicated, but only consider the best articles for publishing on an article marketing site. The idea of publishing articles to an article marketing site and having them syndicated or re-used on other sites by other webmasters is done to create one-way links back to your website. If the quality is not there, but the article is certainly something that should be added to your site, just add them to your site using my methods and forget publishing them. Most of your informational articles will be posted and written online right in the WordPress editor.

You are going to make a decision at some point during the writing of this kind of article. It might be, "Man, this is really good." or "Nah, great for my site, but not really anything the general public would like to read". Before you decide one way or the other, consider this. Let's say you were a top programmer in COBOL in your day. Your website has articles about tips and tricks coding COBOL. Your products happen to be a collection of small pieces of code or collections of these small pieces that can be purchased. You might find that the article you are writing is really boring and you would be right, but to a programmer trying to find some shortcuts to some difficult COBOL coding sequences, you are a Godsend. You may want to publish articles with just enough information that the reader will want to visit the author site - your site - to see if there are any more tidbits they can get from you. Then they see, yes, there are more and they can buy it all done for them for a few bucks and be on their way. They may even want to sign up for your newsletter in case you utter another word.

In a specialty niche like this where you are the expert, you will find people will want to read and hear every word you say. It is important to publish some of your really good informational articles on an article marketing directory site because they are directly related to bringing traffic in about your topic. Not all your articles that can be categorized as informational will be published, but the one-way links back to you that are *on topic* as opposed to typical viral articles that may not be on topic at all have an added benefit. On topic viral articles are much more valuable from a search engine standpoint. We are working towards *Web Authority* on a particular topic, remember? It is very important to have some of these type of informational articles published on an article marketing directory site if you have a tight niche like that.

CONCEPT: EARLY CONVERSION FUNNEL.

Informational articles are to be written specifically about the topic that you've chosen. That is why it is very important to have a topic and not write just anything you want in your blog. Topic bridging keeps things related. Pick a topic and stick with it. Informational articles widen the "early conversion funnel". What is an early conversion funnel? For that matter, what is a funnel?

This book is section eighteen of an online product library I built called the Internet Sales Funnel. You can find links to that product throughout this book. A sales funnel is the process that a person unknown to you takes from first discovering your site on the internet to becoming a client. The visitors to your site are your prospects. Many prospects which are the visitors to your site go in the top of the funnel and only a smaller percentage will make a purchase. The smaller percentages are the sales that come out of the bottom of the funnel. There are always many more prospects than sales. The people that buy are your clients. When we refer to an early conversion funnel, we're referring to widening the top of the funnel so that more possible prospects come in the top of the funnel and hopefully, buy sooner. You can widen the funnel at the top by writing more articles that are only informational in nature. People don't like being 'sold' and will avoid reading anything that they think might possibly make them part with their money. By providing useful information without pushy salesmanship, we bring more people who do not necessarily know they need to buy anything to read your article. As they read, some will realize they do need the product you sell. That product just happens to solve a problem they have and you provide the button that allows them to own it.

Let me give you an example. Your site sells kits that have all the pieces, parts, and tools needed to make a certain kind of jewelry. You put this kit together because making jewelry is something you love to do. It has always been a problem for you to get all the items you need. You have to buy one item downtown at a hobby store, one item at an art supply store, and several others online. Making this jewelry is something anybody can do if they knew where to go, but it is a struggle to find all the items they need, especially starting out. You stand ready to make the kit and ship it to them.

You usually buy enough for say five or six kits at a time and you make about fifty percent profit each sale. Not too bad. You need more orders. You have a squeeze page and a blog with product articles for each item. You also have several all-inclusive kits of everything they need with several variations and quantities available to purchase. The payment buttons are all there and anyone coming to your site can order whatever they need. You have a couple clients already and maybe a few reorders, but not enough income. The problem is that you are relying on someone looking for a kit just like yours and people don't know they need this kit. First, you haven't told people how to make this jewelry. Second, some people will never figure out how to make this kind of jewelry. Third, they don't know how much trouble it is to find all the items and tools they need. The bottom line is that your prospective clients do not realize they can make some really cool jewelry out of the items you provide. The income will never increase if you leave things the way they are.

How do you convey that message? How do you build up some excitement? How do you create a need in people for what you sell and ultimately build and increase sales? That is where informational articles come in. Informational articles can come in a number of forms. The basic informational article would talk about a problem and then discuss a solution. The solution is always some product you carry. Let's say that this jewelry needs some special soldering technique to get it just right. Write several articles about how hard it is to solder jewelry and discuss how to do it correctly with the most success. At the end of the article, you suggest that the solder gun you use is exactly what they need. It just happens to be included in a kit or sold separately in your online store, please click here. Do some serious keyword research and find keyword phrases people are already using when they have soldering problems with jewelry. Write articles using the keyword phrase block set of twelve to fifteen phrases you found using my SEO blog writing formula. That is just one aspect of this particular problem that you have a solution for.

Another method is to create some short videos showing your technique using your solder gun. Put the video on YouTube using YouTube tags and make sure you have Google AdSense on your videos. Use *YouTube HTML embed code* to put the video into the articles you wrote or refer them to a link where they can watch the "How To". Or you can put the video on a WordPress post using the *YouTube HTML embed code.* From each of the articles you have written on this particular subject, put links to the article where the video was placed creating more intra-site links. Using this method with several or many keyword phrases used by people to research soldering jewelry, you bring a lot of potential prospects to your site that do not yet know they need your kit. They learn about it, see you do it on a video, and realize they not only want something similar, but they really need it. Be sure to include the "Find out more" link which leads to your payment button. You have effectively widened your funnel and created what I call an early conversion funnel.

Because visitors to your site read your article and find information only, no sales job, they aren't thinking "I'm going to get sold something, something I do not want and do not need". They definitely are not looking for your product. They are just looking for information on a subject they are curious about. The conversion funnel is wider at the top because there is a lot of traffic that is not interested in buying anything. However, they just might buy something once they get there and learn they had a problem and you had a solution. The subject has a clear connection to your company, but not necessarily your product or offer. There is always a call to action whether it is to find out more or to sign up to your newsletter so you can let them know what is new in the world of making jewelry. We're trying to lure them into buying something with informational articles about the product or topic that they are interested in. In this case, the purpose of the informational articles is to provide a service to people interested in making jewelry in return for the opportunity to provide items they need should they have the problems your products solve.

LOVE YOUR TOPIC

Hopefully you are writing articles about a topic that you love, so it is fun. You are talking to people that are also interested in the same topic that you are. It is fun hanging out and sharing ideas with other people interested in the same subject. I need to mention one other method of getting together with your online friends, prospects, and clients. I have an online conference room which I hope you will visit someday. I conduct live online webinars about this book and online marketing in general once or twice a week. Owning your own conference room can be very economical. All you need is a computer and an inexpensive camera with a microphone built in. You may not feel comfortable with public speaking, but if it is a subject you love, most of us can talk about it for hours. There is really no reason to be nervous when it is fun.

Sending email announcements out to the people in your newsletter inviting them to a presentation on how to use that solder gun and answering questions coming from attendees live is an incredibly effective sales tool. If you also offer some sort of incentive to attend, like a discount, you will usually make several sales every time. There are several conference room services I suggest. Google Hangouts allows you to get ten people into a conversation and it is free. There is an add-on product that expands Google Hangout's capabilities called WebinarJam. Another product is available from Global Virtual Opportunities or GVO called GVO Conference. I use both services.

What other kinds of things can be categorized as informational and used like in our example of soldering jewelry? You may have application notes, case studies, industry trends, or white papers. You are sharing with your readers the information that you are gathering. You are providing them a service. Now they have a reason to sign up to your newsletter, to stay abreast of what is happening. You become their source of information. Over time, if you do this right, you become their trusted and most important source of information for your topic. It is an important part of your business. The service you are providing is like an information broker for your topic as the authority on the subject. At some point, you will have achieved *Web Authority.*

Again, that is why it is so important to pick a single topic, a single niche, and stay with it. You cannot be an expert on everything, but you can be an expert on at least one thing, if not several. Pick something to be an expert on, something that you love.

These informational articles are obviously connected or bridged to specific products and the offers are by implication. There is always that call to action. These make great opt-in pieces specifically for article marketing. "For more information or if you want to keep in touch about what is going on in the world of making jewelry at home, sign up to my mailing list. I will make sure you know about it first." They are called opt-in pieces because they are geared towards getting someone to sign up to your newsletter. Almost without exception, auto responders all require people who sign up to opt-in twice. It is what called double opt-in. They put their name and email into a webform on a webpage and press a submit button. That is the first opt-in. Then they have to look for an email from you and click on the link provided. That is the second opt-in. It is the accepted non-spam way to add people to your list. These informational articles help build your list.

Informational articles have excellent ranking benefits as well. These are not generally going to go viral, but they assist in broadening the types of long tail searches that people might find you with. Each one of the articles you write are going to be search engine optimized my way in order to bring you traffic. The informational article traffic is higher quality because it is specifically targeted for your particular subject or topic.

MUCH MORE ON VIRAL ARTICLES

Viral content is primarily written to be syndicated. Remember, syndicated means these articles are to be published on an article marketing directory site, Syndication occurs when other webmasters re-publish your article on other websites. They are an art form. It takes a little research and some help from friends to model an article that will be passed around to the extent that it can be called viral. What does viral mean? Think about this. We all pass on jokes, interesting articles, movie clips, or other pieces of information that we think our friends, families, or co-workers should see. Sometimes we pass them on to just a few people we know, but if it is really good, we will pass it on to everyone in our mailing list. We might even re-post it to Facebook or tweet about it. In turn, some of the people we pass it on to will also pass it on. A really good viral article can literally circle the world many times and still be circling years later. Imagine the links you could get from something like that.

Do you need something to go that crazy? Fortunately, the answer is no. If it just goes a little viral and gets passed on a little bit, say within a specific industry to some of the important players; that would be sufficient. Viral articles usually do not have much to do with our own topic and they don't get us much traffic either. You're trying to maximize the number of links you get back to your site. The search engines are looking for traffic and links. We have to do something to generate links to our site. The best way it turns out is a viral article.

It takes some thought to come up with something that will go viral. It has to be good enough that someone would want to pass it on to another person. It has to be good enough that someone would believe that a friend or colleague would benefit from receiving it. It can also just be funny and accomplish the same goal. A site like www.google.com/trends/ can give you new ideas about what folks are discussing. http://www.ezinearticles.com also provides trends based on what people are writing and asking about.

Here's an example of something I'd like to see. I would not know how to get this filmed, but it would be absolutely hilarious. Remember kitten herding? Take as many pictures and short movie clips from as many angles as you can. You cannot force funny, but this would be a pretty good shot at it. Edit the clips and pictures together, add some cool music and now you have a viral video. I know I would pass it on.

Another idea is to capture what people do at different times of the year, perhaps about what a particular holiday means to them. I have seen Power Point presentations with beautiful photos and awesome music. Post the presentation on YouTube or your website. Write an article using the presentation and post it on an article marketing directory site and start sharing the link. Ask others to share it as well. Some people add phony claims that your whole life will fall apart if you do not pass it on to at least 10 people. We've all received these at least one of those in our lifetime. These will create links, but stay away from the warnings of doom. You get the idea.

By the way, do you realize that with Google AdSense, every five people that visit your YouTube channel and watch your video, even if it is ridiculous like something I just mentioned, that you get a penny? So, for every 100,000 people that look at it, you get five grand in your pocket. Can you imagine what a million hits will be? Do you realize some people are making a very good living making movies like this?

Look around on YouTube some time. You will know Google AdSense is in play if you have to skip an ad to see what you want to see. After the video, go to YouTube where it is hosted, and look at the statistics for that video and do the math. In most cases, these people will have a channel with many videos. Each one of their videos gets many views. It all adds up. Some people are making a nice income entertaining people with funny viral videos, playing cover tunes, or singing Karaoke using Google AdSense. You have to say to yourself, "Can I do that?" Well yes, you can. It does not have to go crazy viral to be of tremendous benefit to you.

Remember that a viral article does not need to have anything to do with your particular topic. The Bacon distance can be as far as you want. Viral articles do not bring you much traffic, but they will create links to your site. Let's say I'm a reader and I read your funny article out on some article marketing directory site like ezinearticles.com. I laughed and thought, how clever, who wrote this? So I check out who you are. I click on the link on the published viral article and I'm taken to a page that hopefully you put together just for visitors that read your viral article. It might read something like this; "Hey, I hope you love that video. I put that together and had an absolute blast with it. I may come up with another one very soon. Do not miss out. If you add your name and email to my mailing list, I will make sure you are notified as soon as it is available."

You will have a few readers that do not care about your topic on your list. Maybe they just do not know they are interested yet. Over the next year, you are going to be sending an email occasionally about a new article you wrote and include information about new products you have. Some of them will be interested. Having these people add themselves to your list is just a bonus.

WHY YOU WANT TO GET LINKS THIS WAY AND NOT OTHERS

What if you wrote a particularly funny article that everybody passed around; a totally original article that was just awesome? You published it on an article marketing site and it has been syndicated. Other webmasters have added it to their own sites and you've gotten a lot of links from it. Maybe it wasn't incredibly viral, but you earned five hundred authority-ranked links back to your site with this one article. Do you know how long it takes to get that many if you want to do this some other way?

Another way to get links is to do swaps; "Hey, I will give you a link if you give me a link." Each of these links requires a conversation, several emails, or a phone call. Then you have to edit your page to include their links. Then you have to double check constantly because people will take the links off after a while. Can you imagine how long that takes? If links are so important to page ranking, I submit to you that having conversations with five hundred other webmasters to swap a link is an awful way to go about it. And swapped links are reciprocal links and not as good a quality as being the final destination of a one-way link.

VIRAL TOPICS

What kind of topics can you use for a viral article? The topic bridge can be sketchy if non-existent. In other words, the Bacon distance can be largely ignored. It's great if you can write a viral article that matches the topic of your site, but if you are just starting out, don't worry about it. The topic of the article can have absolutely nothing to do with your website or products. Popularity is the main concern. You aren't writing an article for yourself here, you are writing it to satisfy the masses. You will get very little traffic from an article like this and what little traffic is generated will be poorly targeted. The bottom line is you can write about any topic you want.

THE REJECT PILE

No matter how good a writer you are, there are going to be a few articles that are more suited for the reject pile. No writer starts out to write junk, but it happens. The temptation is to use them anyway. Let me caution you, fix it first. Make the article acceptable. Edit them until they are good enough for your gold standard or throw them out.

SUM IT UP

You need all three types of articles, product articles, informational articles, and viral articles to be successful. Product articles are one step removed from the sale itself. You should have a minimum of two product articles for every item you are selling. You need Informational articles. You need a minimum of two informational articles for every product that you have or that you carry. I say minimum here because I want you to get started right away. You can always build on your success later, but you have to start somewhere so the money starts coming in. Afterwards, you will be adding more and more informational articles. Lastly, you will need viral articles. You only need a few very good ones for as many links as you need.

Here is an example. You are about ready to launch your site. Your sales funnel is almost complete. Let's say you have ten products. That means you should have twenty product articles for those ten items, each one leading to a payment button. You also have 20 informational articles about your topic that all have a call to action which is either to review the product articles or add the reader to your newsletter. You have joined an article marketing directory site and have published a couple of viral articles. You have a squeeze page done with your auto-responder. You are ready to rock and roll. That is the basic minimum I suggest before you start actively marketing your site.

There is a lot more to Internet marketing and this book is only section 18 of my huge library of online webinars. I urge you to visit http://www.Internetsalesfunnel.com for more information and other methods of traffic generation.

So what about moving forward from here? You have all this done, but you haven't done a new article for a little while. Everything's working pretty smoothly. That is a danger. If you are standing still, you are falling behind. Remember I said, at least in Google's blog search engine, you need to write an article once a week for Google to remember you exist? You need to write new articles once a week, either informational articles or a viral article.

What else? Let's say you pick up a new product. You will want to add a couple articles into your blog and a couple new emails into your autoresponder at a minimum. After that, if no new products are added, you keep writing informational and/or viral articles at least once a week. As you add articles to your blog you can copy portions of those articles into an email that you are going to put in your auto-responder. The email serves to entice them to come back to your site to read the article.

ARTICLE PERCENTAGES

Informational articles should be about 50% of the content on your site, but that can grow the longer you work your site. This is your long tail SEO content. That means that this content is meant to capture traffic from as many keyword phrases as we can write for. Viral articles will be much fewer at ten percent. The viral content is going to be the majority of your links that are coming in from other sources. The product articles will be the rest of the total percentage of articles, two or more for each item. The product articles are going to remain fairly static in number depending on the number of items you sell. The percentages will vary depending on the age and size of your site. This should give you a rough idea of what your blog and site should look like.

BRIDGING PATTERNS

What happens when you have a product that is not necessarily a match for your particular topic? As we've seen, it is a match if you want to make it a match. In other words, how do you bridge the topic so that you have that endless amount of content to match back to your site?

Here's an example. I have a site called http://www.advertiseyourbusinessnow.com. It has slightly more than twelve thousand members as of the writing of this book. It is just an advertising system. You can place a free ad and advertise your offer. It is not a business. It is a tool that allows you to market your product. The problem is that advertising is not your product or topic at all and now you are an affiliate. You wouldn't mind making a few commissions if you could from this advertising site. How does one do that?

Let's suppose your topic is about daytime TV and you've figured out a way to monetize a few add-on television gadgets with stories about what is going on today on a soap opera. What does an advertising system have to do with daytime TV? The answer is nothing at all.

You have to get the word out to people somehow. You have to advertise. So even though your site does not have anything to do with advertising, you build a bridge. "Hi, I've been out here talking about daytime TV which is my passion. One of the tools I've been using to let people know about what I am doing is this system called Advertise Your Business Now. This is what it is done for me ... blah, blah, blah. Click here if you want more information." It is short and sweet.

If you've joined a site like *Advertise Your Business Now* or any other advertising site, you probably became an affiliate whether you wanted to or not. You might as well add it to your existing funnel. You want to add two additional product articles about this advertising product using a topic bridge the way that I just explained in the example to your site. You also want to have a couple of follow up emails in your autoresponder. Take some excerpts out of your articles that you wrote. The emails should give just enough text to invite the reader to visit the site for the rest of the article. Do the articles first and then the emails. Add a call to action with a P.S. in your email that says "P. S., by the way..." Give them a little info about what is coming up or a "how-to" do something tip, and then add: "If you are interested in finding out one of ways that I've been able to grow my business, click here to learn about one of the advertising tools that I've been using." That click takes them to the article which has a lot more information with another call to action which leads to your affiliate page for the product in question. You are done. You shouldn't have to do anything more for any product that is just a tool.

This kind of thing is different, but similar to the approach you will take with your core products. This is what I mean when I say to bridge a topic from something that may not have that much to do with your topic, but needs to be a part of your business. Always find a bridge that comes back to your topic.

WHAT SHOULD I WRITE TODAY?

When we start to think about an article to write, we first have to come up with the idea for the article. It starts with the bridge. You might be thinking that we should be starting with keyword phrases. When you actually write the article, yes, you do start with the keyword phrase, but you should already have chosen the bridge. You use the bridge to find some keyword phrases. Then you write the article. You can't choose keyword phrases without having a topic to write about. The bridge may change a little after doing some keyword phrase research, but the topic is what we start with. As we've seen, in order to have endless content or to cover a particular unrelated product we sell, we need to choose a bridge. Now that you have chosen a bridge and decided what kind of article to write today, will this be a product article, informational article, or a viral article?

BRIDGES

Let's discuss bridge width. Informational bridges maximize the quality of traffic. They are designed to bring in traffic first. The bridge is narrower because they only touch on your particular topic in most cases. That means the Bacon distance is small. Viral bridges give us links to our site. Viral bridges can be very wide. That means the Bacon distance can be pretty far. Viral bridges maximize the quantity of linking, but the traffic may be non-existent. Both of those are required to build a well-rounded site that will score well in the search engines.

We also have product articles, but these are very narrow in scope and once we have a few per product, we usually do not need any more unless we see in the future that a particular item is selling very well. So let's say we have had our site functioning for a while now. That would mean we're now just talking about whether we want an informational or viral article.

Let's go informational this time. We need more traffic. By the way, there are tools to determine how many links you have and how much traffic you have called analytics. Analytics are beyond the scope of this book, but let us just say you need to know how many links and how much traffic you have before you can make an educated guess on what to do next. http://www.Alexa.com is a great place to find that information about your website. For now, we have decided we're ok on the links. We need more traffic. We're going to bridge for quality traffic. We're going to write an informational article today.

The article needs to have a reasonably clear connection to your offer; a smaller Bacon distance, so to speak. Some of these informational articles you are going to publish and try to have syndicated and some of them you are not. Once we have an idea of what we're going to write about and what kind of article it is going to be, we need to spend some time doing some research to figure out what keyword phrase we are going to use. We want a phrase that has lower competition and is related to what we're talking about. If we do that, when somebody actually comes to our site, we will have that opportunity to sell our products.

THE MAGICAL SEARCH TERM

We have to continually be on the lookout for search terms that might suit our venture. The subject of finding search terms, what they are, what they do, how they rank can fill volumes - and it does. I'm going to try and break this down for you as simply as possible. You might be asking why you need to know this to write an article. The answer is that you do not need it to write the article, you need to know something about the art of search terms and search engine optimization to maximize your efforts at attracting traffic to your site. The two go hand in hand. If all you want to do is write, that is awesome, but if you cannot get the right search terms covered with articles the way I'm teaching, then you may be the only person that ever reads them. The whole purpose of this book is to make sure the huge effort you put in to making sure your blog is always new and exciting and packed with awesome information about your topic is not wasted. It is a lot of work to create *Web Authority* in such a way that traffic from people searching for things on the Internet ends up on your site more often than your competition. Once you get things going, you can coast a little just maintaining your momentum, but it is work. It does not magically happen on its own. The last thing I will add about this is to remind you that the methods in this book are about free traffic, not paid traffic. Anyone can get paid traffic, although it can be an art not to spend huge sums and still be effective. My methods teach you to be able to create some percentage of targeted free traffic coming to your site every day. That is the magic of search terms and why it is worthwhile to study this book and really understand what I'm trying to teach.

What is the magical long tail search term anyway? By now, you've realized how much searching on the Internet has changed over the last four or five years. These days you can hardly find anything without typing in 4 to 6 words and that is just beginning to narrow the search. The exceptions to this rule are the very odd and strange things that are very unique. If you have strange and unique topics and products, that is awesome, but most of us do not have that advantage. Keyword phrases you choose should be four to six words and sometimes as many as nine. With 2 words, the combinations of words and phrases are small. With three there are more, but at six words, the combinations are quite large, even exponential. With six word phrases, you will even find searches on keyword phrases that nobody is using for their SEO. You will know these because very few choices are returned and the ones that are returned aren't even close to what you are looking for. Note those down, it is an opportunity. I call these holes or gaps. It would be good to do some research on that keyword phrase to see if you can make use of it. These are easy to rank for page one.

The research consists of typing in the phrase to see what is returned. Is there tons of competition? If you add another word, does that change anything? Type it in as a question. Does that change it? After investigating, you will find a phrase or two that look promising. There is a lot to choosing keywords, so for now, just follow along. Take one of the phrases and do a search. The search returns one or two items that match the phrase and the other items returned don't seem to be related. It happens all the time. Google does it's best to display anything closely related. The next thing to find out is whether there is any traffic coming in on that phrase. For this, you use a tool from a search engine like the one available from Google AdWords. You find that there are a thousand hundred hits a month on this phrase. What you've found is a keyword phrase that has virtually no competition, but people are indeed using that phrase to search for items. One thousand hits on this search term may not seem like a lot, but you stand a very good chance of owning most of those hits if you do the SEO work properly.

Hopefully the phrase is on your topic in some manner.

You just found one of the first twelve to fifteen keyword phrases for your block of articles. A keyword phrase with sufficient traffic and little competition is what I call a search engine hole. This is one simple example of the thought process that goes into writing each article. We started with the bridge which was our topic. We did a little keyword research. Once we have the keyword phrase, we write out article using my secret. The last chapter goes much more in depth into just exactly how to write the article to maximize the article's search engine and keyword compatibility.

Some SEO History

When websites were first possible, you had to build your own pages using some kind of editor. There wasn't even an HTML editor to use in the early days. Windows Notepad and an FTP (file transfer protocol) program to move the files up and down from the website was all we had. In the early days you built your own webserver right on your own desktop. Doing a search during this time was not possible. There were no search engines yet. You had to know what the website domain name was. Mostly there were bulletin boards and FTP sites where you could download software drivers and utilities from different manufacturers. Sometime in the 80s, Prodigy came out. It was the first time anything resembling the Internet as we know it was possible. Prodigy ultimately failed, but the idea was planted and stuck. Search engines came along a few years later. The point to all of this is that some corporate websites have changed very little since they got started. Yes, the look and feel has improved and of course major companies like Microsoft and IBM have very vibrant, very important sites. I'm talking about the typical mid-size company with upper-management that after all these years is still not very technical. Many corporations have put little effort into making their websites search engine friendly. Let me explain.

All websites have a default page. It is called the index page. It will be usually index.html or index.php, depending on the technology used by the web server. I've seen this many times. The index page is the only page that some companies do any SEO work to at all. We're talking about the Meta tags in the backside HTML of the page. The title, the description, and the keyword phrases (TDK). These Meta tags tell the search engines what the website is about and where it should be indexed. Do not get me wrong, a lot of companies are figuring this out, but they still haven't done every single page on their website. Your secret is to do a better job than the competition.

Another Secret

I will tell you a secret. When you build a page and choose keyword phrases, some companies will add twenty five or more keyword phrases. This does not work either. It is really, really hard to optimize any page for the Internet for more than one keyword phrase at a time. Let me say that again, it is very, very difficult if not impossible to optimize a page for a search engine for more than one keyword phrase. This is why blogs are so awesome. They allow you to rank every article for one keyword phrase and you can write as many articles as you want.

Let's look at a mid-sized corporation. They have one page for one phrase and they may rank very high. Maybe they even get a lot of traffic. The problem is they are missing so much more. Many of them are not paying attention. The ones I've worked with as a consultant just do not want to spend the money and do not think it will make any difference. It is very short-sighted and old school. Companies I've talked to think about and talk about marketing on the Internet, but doing SEO work is the last thing they think about. They do not understand it so they haven't done anything about it. They had their website built some years ago. They spent the money and they haven't done a thing since. When I ask them if they want some help, they tell me, "Oh no, we got it." Trust me - they do not have it.

It is true that there are a lot of the larger companies have become more educated. They are trying to update their site regularly and even hiring Internet marketing managers. You might think you could never compete with them as a little guy. What I'm trying to point out is that in many cases the Internet levels the playing field for the little guy.

Many companies are absolutely dependent on Google AdWords and pay-per-click paid advertising. They do all their advertising this way and they pay handsomely. Let them. You do not have to spend that kind of money to get the kind of targeted traffic you need. You can compete with them and win. Some big companies I've seen have optimized only main menu pages. That means you are only competing for those few keyword phrases. The irony is that huge companies with hundreds of pages use only a few keyword phrases.

Here you come to market armed with this book. You have a blog. You add this little plugin that allows you to optimize every single article. When you create your article, there is a place for your title, description, and keyword phrases. You've followed my secret formula for optimizing the page. Once you've done the research and know what keyword phrase you want to write about today, you will use that phrase as your title. You are going to use it a couple of times within the body of your article. Maybe you take those keyword phrases, highlight them, and create a link to another article. You will use the keyword phrase in the description and finally, that keyword phrase will be one of twelve to fifteen phrases in your keyword phrases that will be in the area provided for keywords. You will also use those twelve to fifteen keyword phrases as the tags for the article. That is pretty simple isn't it? If you can write twelve to fifteen articles, each using one of those keyword phrases to complete your article block, you can start to command *Web Authority* in the topic covered by those keyword phrases. With your first keyword phrase block, you've already done more than that large corporation with a few optimized keyword phrases. Is this making sense yet?

If you keep this up for one year, one article a week, you will have a website, your blog and all its parts, sitting in the root of your site that has been optimized for fifty-two different keyword phrases. You will be pulling some amount of traffic with each one of them. Your competition will still be out there paying Google AdWords an arm and a leg for a two or three word keyword phrase. It is a tremendous advantage and your competition will wonder what you are doing and why they are losing business to you. If you are a single work-at-home business person, even taking a very small percentage of business from a large player is more than enough for a full time living.

Some companies are starting to get smart, but it is amazing how stubborn some of them can be. Some corporations have an older CEO that does not even have a computer. Some of them couldn't use one if they tried. They have people that do computers for them. When one of their employees comes in and says to them, "We need to allocate this portion of our budget for Internet marketing?" they usually get a push back. "Why do we need that? Back in my day we we're using paper for everything." You may think what I'm saying is silly. That it cannot be true, but I run into it way too much. Companies today understand they must have a web presence, but they usually do not understand marketing on the web at all.

By now, you should see that you really have an opportunity to pick up traffic when nobody else is looking. I do not know how long it will last, but right at this time in history, you do. I predict it will last for at least a few more years. This is why I'm so high on blogs and WordPress only. It may take you nine months to a year to really achieve *Web Authority* on your topic once you get started, but you should still be getting half of your traffic from free searches on the Internet.

Did I mention that one of the reasons for this book is that there is plenty of information on the Internet about how to pay for traffic? The kind of traffic that is free is a lot harder to attract. Nothing in this book is about paying for anything other than the labor involved in creating the content and the monthly cost of hosting your website. Very few are even discussing what I'm teaching. All the "gurus" on the subject are silent.

This is not as true as it used to be, but if you were a light bulb company and you owned lightbulbs.com, you did not have to do any advertising at all on the Internet. You would always come up on the first page in a search engine because you own lightbulbs.com. It is not given as much weight as it used to. There was too much abuse by unsavory webmasters, but it still holds a lot of weight. That is how important keyword phrases are. That is how important these articles are. All we're doing is providing the content with the patterns in them so that the search engines can list us some place where we can pick up traffic.

THE WRONG WAY TO WRITE AN ARTICLE

This is what most people do. They write an article or create a web page. Then they look at the content of the article or page and try to find a decent phrase that should help people find them. They end up optimizing for phrases that have a lot of searches. The phrase may have incredible competition. They did not do any research whatsoever. They just thought that was a pretty good keyword phrase. They may even have gone on the Internet and typed it in and thought they were doing some kind of research. The article itself has a different title and the phrase isn't used in the description or the body of the article. They used the phrase in the list of tags for the blog if they are writing a blog, but they probably do not have a plugin allowing them to rank in Google's regular search engine. They are not aware of what is happening on the Internet and end up trying to optimize their page after the fact for a two or three word keyword phrase.

What are the chances of ranking well for these phrases? Just about nil. Let me explain a bit more. This is important. What if you paid for advertising on your products? Here's the problem with advertising on Google AdWords that people do not understand. Imagine you have a net to catch prospects and create clients. The net is your sales funnel. You try and bring as many prospects into the top and the sales come out on the bottom. A much smaller percentage of all the prospects that enter in the top become buyers out the bottom. You can either make the net really wide or you can make it very narrow by the type of keyword phrase that you choose. If you choose a two or three word or even a four word keyword phrase, your net is pretty wide. If you choose five or six words, you are narrowing your net. The more specific you become by adding words to your keyword phrase, the narrower the net. A wide net may sound like a good thing, but if you are going to pay for a lot of clicks from people that have no idea why they got to your site and they certainly aren't interested, it is dangerous to your finances. You have to pay for those clicks. It gets very expensive very, very fast. So fast that it will make your head swim. In order to make a paid ad campaign work, you will need to really narrow your funnel down by using keyword phrases that are very specific. The amount you make in sales has to exceed the amount you pay for the ads or it is a losing proposition.

Contrast what you have to do with paid advertising with what you might do with just a blog with articles designed to pull in as much free organic traffic as you can. You can widen your funnel considerably. It does not cost anything. But if you widen it too much, you are competing with all those big companies that haven't edited their keyword phrases lately. What is the right answer? It takes some research and a little trial and error and it all depends on the industry and the products you will be carrying. The strategy here is to allow the net to be a little bit wider, while still being quite specific with the keyword phrases you are using. That is why I like my phrase block strategy. Blanket twelve to fifteen keyword phrases at a time and cover as many bases as you can. In this way you widen the funnel by using twelve to fifteen related keyword phrases for a particular product or topic and it still does not cost anything.

That is why I keep suggesting a WordPress blog in the root of your website. It is infinitely better at allowing you to add as many articles as you want, all of them optimized for a particular keyword phrase. Use blocks of articles for a particular topic and have them all picking up traffic and creating *Web Authority*. We are talking specifically about the free searches or organic traffic. What is significant about organic traffic is that it is targeted. What that means is that they were looking for you and they found you. They are actually interested in your product or service and are much more likely to buy. Any other kind of traffic is just noise. Free traffic is almost all organic targeted traffic.

What is a targeted lead? A targeted lead is somebody who actually needs what you are selling and finds you. If you have what they want at a reasonable price, you make a sale. Targeted leads are like money in your pocket. The people that visit your website will be the right people and that means profit.

When we're talking about free traffic, you can use a little wider funnel at the top, but not too wide. There might be fewer visits taking place with a tighter net, but there will be less competition. Your leads will be more targeted, and you have a much better chance at ranking well in the search engines.

INFORMATIONAL BRIDGE PATTERNS, SPACE, TIME, ACTIVITY, OTHER PRODUCTS

Bridging in space

What do I mean by space? When we're talking space, we're talking about the physical location. If you were talking about dog leashes for example, the bridges would be where physically one would use a dog leash. You would write articles about public parks and dog parks. You would write about a city ordinance policy that might have been changed because dogs were not on a leash in public spaces. If you were talking lawns, the space bridge would be where lawns are grown. Where did lawns originally come from? What strange places might you find a lawn like these new green houses that have a lawn on the roof? You could talk about which type of grass grows better where and why.

A person I knew had an awesome idea. This was one of those things that people kept asking for. She got a piece of glass and made a frame for it. She would paint with see-through glass paint. She painted sea creatures, whales, dolphins, and seals on the glass. You could mount it on the fence outside in your yard. It dresses up your garden. The space bridge would be all the great places you could put one of these pieces of art.

Another person I work with sells WordPress plugins. The space bridge in this case is more subtle. It goes into a blog into a specific place. The articles show how to and how to install it and to configure it. But more importantly, what does the landscape look like where you might use one of these plugins? Where does it work best and in what location?

Bridging in time

Bridging in space was primarily about location. Bridging in time is all about when. When is the product used? What kind of event occurs and when does it happen? Does it change over time? Let's use our WordPress plugin example. There is a certain point of time during the construction of a WordPress website where you are going to want to install a plugin. When is a good time to do it? Is there a particular phase of the project as you are building your blog when it is particularly advantageous? If this plugin has a consideration that is time sensitive, this is one of the areas you want to make sure there is an article block. You might want to write about the future of this plugin. Write about the history of this plugin. When traditionally was it used? When is it used now? What was the progression over time in its use?

Bridging in people

Who uses this product? What kind of person is going to use this plugin? It is going to be a WordPress blog owner? I'd say that is obvious. Other people who want to have this ability or that feature of the plugin may not have thought about having a blog at all before now. They may want to consider it now based on your recommendations. They have to understand why they need your plugins. You can write about personal attributes or characteristics of the typical blog owner. You might even get funny about it. It is a big market. What are people doing when they come across a blog that has this plugin installed? What is it going to do for both the blog owner and the people that come across the site while surfing? What kind of person might come across a site like this and use the new feature?

Bridging in activity

What are the activities a blog owner might be involved in that would necessitate the need for such a plugin? What might the activities be of a person who would be interested in acquiring this feature on their site? Would there be specific activities a prospect might be involved in that would necessitate the use of such a plugin? What other activities does this plugin relate to? What is a prospective buyer doing when they come across a blog with this plugin installed?

Bridging other products

What other products are related to this plugin? Maybe you sell several kinds of plugins. If someone purchases one of the plugins, they might be interested in another. Which of these would be related and work together? Are there other products that might be used with the plugin that would make someone who was using one be interested in another one? What else could they buy from you? Have you thought about selling products in packages as well as each one separately? If you have this plugin, then logically you need that one. Click here. Buy that one too. If you describe why that other plugin coupled with this plugin do this and that job well together, then you are going to sell them both.

Write about what products should not be used with this plugin. What other products are your competition? What other plugins do exactly or something similar to what this one does? What is the difference? Why is yours better? Know your industry and know your product. How are those products used together? There are a lot of areas that you can expand on and write about.

All of these types of articles and all the bridging lead to sales. They are just informational articles about plugins. There is no push. There is no heavy sales job. They just tell the reader something about the topic, product, or service. At the end, there is always a call to action. For more information, click here. That click leads to a sales page and the opportunity to own it.

COUNTER INTUITIVE DIVERGENCE – THINKING OBLIQUELY

Here's another concept that will help you find search phrases that may have a lot less competition and enough traffic to help you site rank higher. This goes along with the block strategy where you choose twelve to fifteen search phrases and write articles using my SEO formula for writing blogs for each phrase.

Say you sell dog leashes. You're trying to find the right search phrases for your site and your articles. Most people would choose "dog leash" as their search phrase and spend thousands on paid advertising trying to compete with large pet supply companies. You will lose that battle before you even start. Do a search yourself on Google. Do a search on the two word phrase "dog leash". I came up with over three and a half million options to choose from. Amazon and PetSmart were number one and two. Two word keyword phrases just aren't enough words. Remember, keyword phrases with seven words in them that also have 'dog leash' in them are also being returned as part of that three and a half million. If you want to stand out and have any chance at all among all the noise, you need to think obliquely. It is counter intuitive. Think about how to get prospects to your product from a different direction.

Think about it this way. Write about the kinds of problems a dog leash solves? The potential buyer has a problem. Their dog is pulling hard every time they go for a walk. They might get on their computer and enter "my dog pulls his leash". More than likely, they will ask the question. "How do you keep a dog from pulling when taking them for a walk?" I do not know about you, but it is so hard finding things on the Internet so I usually type in the entire question just like I was standing in front of you. I get much better results.

This is interesting. If you type in "my dog keeps pulling my arm off", Google returns no paid ads at all. That means no sellers have used Google AdWords to advertise this particular phrase. There is very little to no competition for this phrase. There is only one article specifically addressing the issue and several related ones. You will need to do a little research. It starts with having a Google AdWords account. You need access to their keyword planning tool. You do not have to place an ad to use the tool, but you will have to have an account. Go to http://www.adwords.google.com for more detail. Use the keyword tool and enter "my dog keeps pulling my arm off" to find what variations are being used and to find the search volume. You are looking for twelve to fifteen related search terms for your article block that have a fair amount of search volume and as little competition as possible. Remember, your competition is not the store down the street when it comes to the Internet. Your competition is the person who owns the site out there that does a better job of search engine optimization than you.

I did a little research on "my dog keeps pulling my arm off" and here's what I found.

Keyword	Avg. Monthly Searches
stop dog pulling on lead	260
how to stop a dog pulling on the lead	260
dog leads to stop pulling	210
stop dog from pulling on leash	210
how to stop your dog pulling on the lead	140
how to stop your dog from pulling	140
stop dog pulling on leash	140

how to stop a dog from pulling on leash	140
how to stop a dog from pulling on a leash	140
how to stop dog pulling on leash	140
how to stop your dog pulling	110

Here are eleven long tail keyword search terms from five to nine words in length that people actually are using as search terms according to Google. If you optimize eleven articles for each phrase, you stand a very good chance at becoming page one in each of these phrases and receive a good portion of whatever traffic is available. These phrases are so specific that if a prospect reads your article and the perfect solution to the problem is available at a reasonable price, you stand the best chance of making a few sales.

Prospects that are typing very specific phrases are doing research on a real problem they are having and are highly targeted prospects. These phrases may not have thousands of searches every month, but every one of the prospects using these phrases is motivated to find a solution to their problem. They will only read your articles because the solution they need is discussed. Your leash or a leash like it solves the pulling problem. If they are tired enough of the pulling and the price is reasonable, they will buy.

What about a technical product like a WordPress plugin product? People will buy a plugin or any technical product like that because it solves a problem. You need to write about what the problem is. Readers need to be able to read that article and say, "You know, that is exactly what I need. That is what I've been looking for." It is your responsibility to make sure that your product or service is listed in such a way that a search engine can find it. When a prospect has a problem they cannot solve and can get the problem fixed, they will love you for it. If you write a block of articles around this problem using twelve to fifteen keyword phrases properly optimized for the search engines, you will accomplish just that.

Let's take another real world example in a more typical sales environment. When you walk into an appliance store, you have a problem. Most people do not walk into an appliance store just to look around. You have clothes to wash and your washing machine is broken. You are looking for a washer. You find a salesman in the store to help you find a washer that you can afford that does what you need it to do. The salesman is going to talk to you about the features of the washer and ask you questions about your particular washing habits to determine the best fit. You will appreciate the help if this is a great salesman. That is what sales is all about. The *art of sales* is warmly and helpfully solving problems for people. When you have a plugin like we were discussing, it does a very specific job. What problem does the plugin solve for you? That is what you need to be writing about.

Here is something that I notice quite often with new salespeople selling a technical product. If you are new and trying to build a business from home, you will be asked to become an affiliate for this product or that product. For those of you that have been around, you should already know this. I caution you to stay focused on your own product. People you talk to will be trying to get you to focus on them instead of what you should be. You may say yes and try to do a little advertising for this product that you have become an affiliate for. The problem is that you may not know much about this new product or what it actually does. That is another caution. If you do not have time to learn it well enough to sell it, forget it. You must know your products intimately. You need to know everything there is to know about them. You are representing the products just like the appliance salesman. To a prospective client, you are the expert. How many appliances do you think that salesperson would sell if they couldn't even answer the basic questions about each appliance? If it were me, I'd ask for another salesperson or the boss. How about you?

If you are selling a product on the Internet from your home, especially a technical product, you are the one these clients are going to contact for support. That should be scary for you. If something does not work right or breaks, you need to be prepared to help them rectify the problem or find them somebody who can. Otherwise you will be issuing a credit and giving yourself a bad name. Do not go there.

Viral Content
Viral content is different than the informational article. Viral articles aim to bridge for links, not traffic. We do not expect that much

traffic from this, but what we are expecting is to get lots of incoming links. Over time we want our site to become the *Web Authority* site. We want to be the *Web Authority* in our niche. Hopefully, Google keeps finding us at the end of the trail. Most all viral type articles are meant to be published and syndicated.

The key to a great viral bridge topic has to be its wide appeal. It is not what you want to write about, it is what readers want to read. And if you strike a chord with people for something with wide appeal, you will find your article will be syndicated quite a lot. When I say viral, yes, it would be nice to get one and a half million webmasters re-posting your article with those awesome links back to your site. If you can make that happen, you do not need to worry about any more viral articles. That is plenty of links, but I will tell you that thirty or forty per article is not bad. If you want to get a lot of links, write a great viral article that at least people in your industry will distribute, and publish, and syndicate. You might find you get these thirty or forty links in three to five months after writing the article. That is a lot of links and you did it with one article. Is every article going to do that? I'd say probably not. But if you keep at it, the numbers will grow. My point is that links are hard to get any other way and extremely time consuming to trade with other webmasters one link at a time. Writing a great viral article designed to appeal to a wide audience and having it re-posted (syndicated) significantly shortens the time and effort to get enough links to rank well in the search engines.

RECAP

Remember when we started talking about the different kinds of articles we'd need to write? We said we needed product articles, two for each item. These are very specific to each item's features and benefits, with a payment button. Then we need informational articles. These bring the traffic. With these, we will do blocks of twelve to fifteen articles over time for twelve to fifteen keyword phrases using our divergent thinking covering problems that our products solve or just about our topic. The topic is related to what kinds of products we carry. All of these lead to a product page with calls to action and ultimately, payment buttons. Lastly, we need links. The viral articles are designed to mostly be published on an article marketing site. The more they are syndicated or re-published by other webmasters, the more links we get. The more viral, the more links we will receive. We only need as many of these as we need links. We do not expect much traffic from an article like this. The goal is to maximize the links.

ARTICLE RELEVANCE

Relevance is irrelevant to ranking when it comes to viral articles. Google has numerous topic-sensitive patterns, but results show Google does not use them. If you think about it, trying to match the topic to their keyword phrase used in a link is more than artificial intelligence on a web crawler computer offers today. With the incredible number of websites in the world, it is just not possible for a web crawler to figure out that you wrote - the words and the patterns, -make any coherent sense to some computer that does not have much more than a split second to think about it. At the moment, it would be way beyond a super computer's capability. Even so, Google is working on ways to figure this out and eventually they will. If you can relate the viral article back to your topic in some way, it is much better than not relating to your topic at all, but it is not always possible. This applies to viral articles only.

For the time being, writing a relevant viral article is irrelevant. It's because these are published on an article marketing directory and not in your blog. What matters is link and text. The link comes from an area provided in every article marketing website that has the link back to you. You want a keyword-rich link in the resource box for your article. You want to get it published and have it spread as widely and as often as possible, that is to get the article syndicated as often as possible. These are fun to write when. The viral articles will be one of the last things you write before launching your site.

Before I move on, I want to cover what NOT to write about when writing a viral article.

OVERUSED TOPICS FOR VIRAL ARTICLES

1. Sex Topics: This topic is obviously very popular. Most people of any age, male or female, child or adult search on this topic. They

search for stories, toys, videos, photos, comics, animation etc. It is overused and therefore has incredible competition on most of the available keyword phrases.

2. Technology Topics: This topic is searched very frequently by those people who want to be aware of new technology products and their versions and variations. It is also overused although if you do choose to take this route, timing is everything. I suggest only attempting to write articles that are on very new technology. There is always a short window when things are very new.

3. Music Topics: This is another topic which is heavily searched. Again, bands and musicians that have been around a while already have a lot of content available. New bands or breaking news however, may have a short timing window available.

4. Health Topics: This topic has an incredible amount of content and as such, is very difficult to make any headway. Again, there are always new breakthroughs and again, there may be short timing windows where a well-written article may find its place.

5. Celebrity Topics: People are always interested in celebrities and their lifestyles. If you specialize in one or several celebrities, and you follow my directions in creating a block of articles around a particular subject or event surrounding that celebrity, you may be able to make some headway. But the content in this area is already overloaded.

6. Events Topics: Events are the most searchable topics on the Internet because one or more events occur every day. These are very time sensitive and you are competing with every news agency on the planet. If you can find a new angle on an event, you may have some luck.

7. Country and Culture Topics: Many people want to know about other countries and their culture. The content in this area is also overloaded. Where I've noticed some success is with a travelogue done with videos and commentary on specific places of interest that may not be well covered. I've also noticed articles about how to live in another country are of special interest to people who will be visiting or moving to that country. This area is not so time sensitive and articles in this area have better longevity.

8. Sports Topics: Sports will always be very popular. If you were actually at an event and noticed something unusual, you may have an opportunity to break through the cacophony of noise and heavy content about sports teams and athletes. Otherwise, do not bother.

9. Job Topics: Jobs are one of the most searched areas on the Internet and the content is very heavy. Think about the many organizations helping people find jobs, talking about how to find jobs, and what the job market is doing, has done, and will be doing. This is one I just would not bother with.

10. Free Software Topics: Unless you are offering free software yourself, you won't be able to compete on this topic. You may be able to compare different free software and make some headway, but there are so many companies that offer free software and actually do none of the sort. There are pages and pages. You may have seen these sites. A lot of it is chock full of viruses. This is another one I'd stay away from. This is one area Google has done a terrible job in cleaning up the cheaters.

11. Free Games Topics: Children and a lot of adults want to play and download games online and they search every day for a new game and their updates. This area is overloaded, but there is always a short window of opportunity right before and after a launch of a new game.

12. News Topics: News is a very time sensitive subject for the news agencies and every newspaper and magazine on the planet. You need to compete with them to make headway in this area. There is a third major Google search engine which is News based. You will need to work with this search engine to stay abreast of what is going on.

13. Online Education Topics: These topics are heavy on the Internet already and are not time sensitive. You may be able to compete by covering new techniques or educational areas that are unique.

14. How to Topics: This is a tough one. It is covered heavily. There are always new products coming out though and there may be opportunities to write articles on how to use new products. This would also be somewhat time-sensitive. Still, there are many areas that are terribly underserved or fraught with misinformation.

15. How to make Money Topics: This is the OMG topic of them all. Every Internet guru and want-to-be guru is trying to compete in this area and there may be mcre content on these topics than any other. One of the sites I run is an advertising site for home business ventures. I can tell you from experience, the most used keyword phrase is "make money online". There are always new products so you may be able to write a time-sensitive piece on a new marketing strategy or "system". But unless you can find an angle that is truly unique, try to write on other topics.

THE RESOURCE BOX

What is a resource box? It is the most important part of any article to be published on an article marketing directory site. Do not do any kind of syndication or publishing of your article unless you are going to do a resource box - a good one. This is the whole purpose of the article. The resource box has the link back to your site. If you have no resource box, you have no links coming back to your site and you might as well not bother.

Some of you are writing because you just love to write and do not care if anyone ever reads any of it. That is wonderful, but for the vast majority of us, this isn't that fun. We're interested in making money. We're marketing our own sites in order to make a living. You are interested in learning how to do all this article marketing *Web Authority* stuff to bring traffic and links to your site so you can raise your page ranking. You want bring in more traffic, bring in more links, and increase your business the amount of money you make. Before we detail what a resource box is and what should and should not be in one, let's take a short lesson in sales.

THE SECRET TO SALES

You know you are an internet salesperson, right? Maybe all you do is write articles and try to market your products on the Internet and you never talk to anyone unless there is a return or a problem with the product. That makes you a non-traditional salesperson, but a salesperson nonetheless. Here's the secret to all sales from way back when - before the Internet - and we will bring it forward to today because it still applies. You may have never heard this before. The secret to making sales is three little words. I learned this from Thom Hopkins, *The Art of How to Sell Anything*. He passed it on from his mentor, J. Douglas Edwards. The words were STP. It means "See the People!" What does that mean? Talking traditional sales back in the day, that meant to talk to as many people as you possibly can. "Sales" has always been a game of numbers. How does that apply today? Instead of seeing people, you let your computer contact people by bringing in traffic. The more traffic you bring in, the more business you do. It really is as simple as that. What makes it a little more complicated is the kind of traffic and what people see when they visit your site. It is not like an earth-shattering secret, is it? One of the ways that you can accomplish bringing in the right traffic and letting people hear what you have to say is by building trust through article marketing the way this book describes it. Okay, now you understand what it is to be an internet salesperson.

An article does not have to go crazy viral. I am not trying to make you think this is so impossible for you to do that you are never going to manage it. Maybe you just cannot seem to get your articles to go viral at all. All you really want is a number of different sites to borrow your article and put it on their site. A few is fine. You will get better over time.

Let me clarify what I mean. The three types of articles that we've been talking about are product articles, informational articles and viral articles. Product articles are closely tied to actual sales, but product articles are not usually suited to bring in much traffic. You have to have them or you won't sell anything. Informational articles bring us traffic. Viral articles bring us links. Using this all around approach, we get the traffic and the links required to rank well in the search engines. When the search engines follow the links, they end up on your site. If the search engines do this enough times, specifically, more than everyone else and for long enough, you become the *Web Authority* site.

The reason I bring all this up one more time is that it leads us back to the resource box. The resource box has the link back to your site. It is required to be maintained by these other webmasters in order to use your article. These are one-way authority based links to the author. The terms and conditions of most of these article marketing sites usually require two things. They require whoever wants to re-publish the article to maintain a link to the author and also a link back to the article marketing site. Whoever uses that article, not just you;

must abide by these rules. This link back to you is what we are trying to achieve.

WHAT WE MIGHT WRITE ABOUT TO MAKE A VIRAL ARTICLE

What do we write about? It is better if the topic is related to our site topic, but the article topic really does not matter. Make it funny, interesting, earth-shattering, make it something that somebody will read and absolutely find enthralling. Try and write it so that other webmasters will want to use it on their own website. Remember who the client is when it comes to writing a viral article for the purpose of re-publishing. Our customers are other webmasters. When other webmasters re-publish our articles, we get the links we're looking for. What makes it viral? Viral is nothing more than something you might pass on to a friend or two. Your friends pass it on to their friends. The article takes on a life of its own. We talked earlier about how viral it needs to be. I would not be too concerned as you get started. Some viralness is enough. Most of us will never write a masterful article that gets re-published around the world. If you write an article today and several weeks later, ten webmasters have re-published your article; that is what you want. Forget about it after that. You will find over time the number of times the article will be re-published will grow. Ten one-way awesome links back to you by writing one article is not bad for the effort. We may never know day to day how Google's search engine algorithm works, but writing one viral article for every block of twelve to fifteen articles will be a good start.

A resource box is in a nutshell; information about the author. The resource box is the most important part of any article that you might get published on an article marketing site, period. It gets you your link. If it gets published without one, your article is worthless as a source of increasing your rankings in the search engines. This is where you promote yourself, your product, and your website. It is better if you do not promote your site in the main body of the article. That practice is prohibited and frowned upon at best. The purpose of an article to be published is to provide good information, not to sell your product. Of course we want to sell our products, but we're going to do that by an overall approach to our marketing. We need links to our site to increase our rankings. That is what the resource box does for us. It is not only an interesting way to get these links we need, but the easiest and most effective.

HOW TO CREATE A RESOURCE BOX

There are some essential elements of a resource box that you must have. Your name is the first one. This might be your pen name or your real name. It is the name that you are trying to brand. You would be amazed how many people forget that. You also must have a website address. This is that link we have been talking about. Without it, do not bother with all of this.

WHERE DO YOU BRING VISITORS IF THEY DECIDE TO CLICK?

It is up to you, but do not bring visitors that clicked your link from your resource box to just any old page on your blog. These visitors liked your work. They may not be interested in your products if your article is a long Bacon distance away from your topic, but you never know. Don't waste the opportunity.

The typical default setup in WordPress is to show the most current article. If you left it as a default in WordPress, then you are leaving things to chance. I'd take your visitors to a specific page or a particular article. Even better is to write an article that is a catch-all for your viral traffic coming from the article marketing sites. The viral articles you have published will be posted on an article marketing directory site, or re-published by some webmaster. You won't know where the visitor is coming from. Visitors may be other webmasters who are interested in other articles or content you have available. Visitors may just be someone who read the article and are curious about the author. They want to visit your website and find out more about you. A good catch-all article specifically for visitors like this may say something like "Hi, you must have come here from one of the articles that I published. I'm really glad you are here. My website is about et cetera, et cetera. If you would like to receive my newsletter and learn about other articles I'm writing, click here". You now make the visit an opportunity, not just a link. Once they are your mailing list, there is even more opportunity to email them information and offers. This is your "Elevator Pitch". It is one to three sentences that encapsulate the essence of what you are about, what you are offering, and your unique selling proposition. It is also your mission statement.

THE MISSION STATEMENT

A mission statement is important - very important. You must be able to tell your prospects what you are about in a few sentences to grab their attention. What are you all about? What is your topic? One of my students mentioned a software product they were selling. When I asked them for more detail about the software they weren't really sure what the software did. Somebody gave him reseller rights to sell this software. When I asked, "What does it do? Why does it do it? What do I need it for?" He really couldn't tell me. I wasn't interested because I couldn't tell what it would do for me either. You need to know what you are selling. If you do not know what it is, how are you going to tell anyone else?

How many times do people just getting started do things like this? To them, this new product looks like the next bright shiny object and they think they are going to make a big killing on the market. The reality is that they have no idea what they are doing. You should be much more wary. Test it yourself. Say you become an affiliate or you acquire reseller rights, and you start selling this new product. You're very excited. You do some marketing and spend time and money. Later you find out that for one, the commissions stink. Two, it is really a difficult product to sell. Worse yet, it's out of date and does not exactly do what it advertises it's supposed to do. Maybe it is buggy and causes you more phone calls and heartaches than you ever wanted. It could happen. The result of all your hard work and effort ends up being you've hurt yourself and your reputation.

It takes so much time and so much effort to build your list and reputation that recommending something that you did not test, or at least making it obvious to people that you have no idea how it works can be very dangerous. People add themselves to your list because they trust you, they like you, and what you've been telling them is right.

What is your mission statement? How can you quantify in a few sentences your unique selling proposition, your mission statement? There is not much room to write. Last time I looked, on ezinearticles.com, there was a limit of 300 words for your resource box. You only have a couple of sentences to say what you are all about. A mission statement is something that you have to think about for a while. It is something that you need to pin to your wall, look at it, and revise it until you like what it says. It is serves as a roadmap so you know where you are going. It keeps you on the straight and narrow path to success. When you are confused or wondering whether this product, or that product is something that you need to get involved in, you can look at your mission statement and think, "This is or is not what I'm about."

Move on. I say this because there is always someone trying to steer you in their direction. They will listen politely to what you have to offer, but what they really want is for you to buy into their offer. You shouldn't care if that person is a best friend or a family member. You have your own direction, and you know where you are going. If it does not help you in your business, stay away from it.

I have worked in a large corporation when somebody in upper management one day realized, "Hey, we do not have a mission statement." A large corporation with thousands of employees who aren't really sure what the company's goals are is not a good thing. Both times I witnessed this process; it took two to three months of study to word in several sentences the mission statement of the company. It had to be a well thought out two or three sentences. When it was finalized, everybody agreed with it. It can take a lot of time.

Let me give you an example of a process I undertook myself for one of the companies I founded many years ago. I wrote everything down and I ended up with about a page and a half. I thought it was great. I asked somebody I trusted for his opinion thinking he was going to pat me on the back and say, "well done". He ripped it to shreds. I was taken aback My pride was hurt. I thought I did a great job. He was right. It was way too long. So I took the suggestions and came back with something that was about half a page. I took it to that same person and he thought it was wonderful. I didn't stop there. I took it to another person I trusted. These were people that I looked up to, that I had either worked for, or owned companies and knew what they were talking about. The next person ripped it to shreds. I ended up doing this three more times. Each time, I had to put my pride aside and move forward. The end result was a three sentence statement. It said much more than my page-and-a-half. It absolutely said all I wanted and more. It was hard, but ever so important. It gave me direction and focus and got me where I wanted to be much quicker. Coming up with a mission statement is not a simple thing. Everybody you show it to will have a different opinion. Just keep your pride in check and the end result will be a focused direction you will be proud of. When you are done, it is not a bad idea to have it up on your wall in front of you so that everyone coming through your doors or visits your website will know what you are about. This statement may should be incorporated into your unique selling proposition and posted on your website where everyone will see it.

As you try and live up to your mission statement, you will be able to stay focused and you will have a sifter to put events and offers through. Does this fit into my mission statement? If it does not, move on.

CALL TO ACTION

Your resource box must have a call to action. It is an opportunity to capture another possible client. You've got them warmed up. They read your article. They like it. Now it is time to lead them to buy or at minimum, add themselves to your newsletter. That is why it is very important to have a link they can click on. Give them something to fill out, like a webform from your auto-responder. Once they complete the double opt-in, thank them and let your autoresponder do its job afterwards. A simple invite might sound something like this; "If you would like more information about me or (your topic), click on this link and complete the form for my newsletter."

OPTIONAL ITEMS FOR YOUR RESOURCE BOX

An optional item to include is your subscription email address. This used to be a common feature of autoresponders, but it has been abused by hackers so it is rare these days. Another item might be additional contact information. I like to include my Skype address. Add a Facebook page or group link. You could add a Twitter, Linked In or Pinterest page. Be careful with too many links though. It may be better to lead them to a page where you provide all of this information. If you have something you can give away like a free report or a white paper, you will find you will get a lot more clicks.

If you have already written a number of articles, take a couple of them, combine them into something coherent, put your name on it, put a logo on it, and there is your free report. **Doc Stone Tip:** Write your own reports. Beware of the "Free eBooks" out there. Maybe somebody's given you the resale rights for a free eBook they wrote. Most of them do not help you and they are usually selling something and it is not your products. Most are PDF files or some kind of file that is difficult to modify, and if you will notice at the very end, there is a call to (their) action or they are selling something. That is why it is free. You just got duped into selling something for someone else when the purpose of this was to sell something for yourself. Take the time to put together a free report and add a link to the end of your resource box with a note that says; "Get this Free Report on "Your Topic", click here." Make them opt-in to your newsletter to get it. There is your call to action.

WHAT NOT TO PUT IN YOUR RESOURCE BOX

We have discussed what you should include in your resource box. What should you *not* include? First, do not include a list of every website you own. That looks unprofessional. If you feel that is necessary, take your prospects to a page where you can list them all. I can see listing many sites if you are a website designer and are trying to highlight your work. If you are not, you really need to pick a topic and stick with it. Besides, once a prospective client signs up for your newsletter, they are now on your list. Over time they are going to get emails about everything you have. All you really want to do is get them on your list with a call to action.

You do not need to put every accomplishment you've ever done in your resource box either. Really, nobody cares. Keep it brief and to the point. Your unique selling proposition should be benefit-oriented. You do not need advertisements or pictures of products that are not relevant to the topic of your article.

Let me clarify one thing before I move on in case some of you missed this earlier. The only kind of article I am suggesting you get published on an article marketing directory site is the viral article. Therefore, only a viral article requires a resource box. Articles written directly into your blog do not require a resource box. The viral article will not pick up much traffic, but it will pick up links. A resource box is the place we can put our link. The link may be clicked on. If it is, we want to take advantage of it. The bottom line is you are not selling anything initially.

One of the things that I often look for are articles on SEO which is search engine optimization. I need to keep abreast of anything going on in the industry. When I see a good article and it sounds like the person who wrote it has some clue what they are talking about, I feel the need to click on the author link with the express purpose of trying to see if I can get on their newsletter. I want to get emails from them. It keeps me informed about what is going on in this industry. I actively look for good sources of information. They are providing a service to me and I appreciate it. If you are providing information that people need, they won't hesitate to add themselves to your newsletter.

Keep the resource box small. It should be no more than fifteen percent of the article. If it is anything bigger, it is considered abusive. As I said earlier, ezinearticles.com enforces the size of the resource box by only giving you enough room for roughly fifteen percent of your article.

AN SEO TRICK

One of the things you will be adding in your resource box is your link. Let's talk about the construction of your link. This is important especially if the article being published is related to the topic for your keyword phrase. Let me give you a good reason. Let me take you on a path as if you were a search engine for a second. Your job is to go digging around on the Internet and categorize and index everything you find. You come across a site that has re-published the author's article. You recognize the use of a particular keyword phrase several times in the body of the article and in the title. You, as the search engine, follow the link to the author. If the topic of the site belonging to the author matches the keyword phrase you are following, then you have found a very powerful authority link which helps the sites rankings.

If you've ever created a link, you know the words and the actual physical URL that a click would take a reader to, that is; the construction of the link can be completely different. You've seen these. The links are usually blue in color and are underlined. When you hold your cursor over these links, your cursor shows you that the link can be clicked. The words you click on and the URL that the link redirects your browser to can be completely different. An example would be when the user clicks on two words <u>Click Here</u>, the browser redirects to http://www.google.com. In the WordPress editor, highlight the words "Click here." Then click the chain link icon. There are 2 fields, enter some text that describes what the link is and the URL will be <u>http://www.google.com</u>. Click Add Link to save. If the keyword phrase you highlighted and the website that the reader is redirected to are related, you get brownie points from the search engines.

So, let's get back to our journey. You, as a search engine, came across an article on this website. You saw a link with the keyword phrase. As a search engine, you are obligated to follow that link to see where it leads you. You are trying to find the original source. If you follow this link and the article you come to is related, and also on topic, you have found the source. If this happens enough times, that site must be the *Web Authority* site. If the article you find has that same keyword phrase as the title and description, it is used in the keyword phrases, used in the tags and used a couple of times in the body, you as a search engine have found a site where a very strong relationship exists between the article and the keyword phrase. We want as many of these strong links as we can get. This is a key concept.

Make your links count. It is okay to have any old link in your resource box, but making it a main keyword phrase for your topic on top of everything else is dynamite. So call it a trick. Call it whatever you want. It is really just basic stuff. The point is to try and think like a search engine. Make a page or an entire website what we call search engine friendly is really just giving the search engines what they want.

A Sample Resource Box

Here is a sample resource box.

"Wendy Writer is a sought-after speaker, international bestselling author, and educator who is passionate about showing business owners and entrepreneurs how to better understand the Internet and to build highly responsive, targeted list of clients specific to their business niche." To receive your FREE special report, "How to Build a Customer List and Get Clients" plus subscribe to receive weekly how-to articles to expand your online Internet toolkit, visit Wendy's website at How to Build a Customer List and Get Clients

Do you see the unique selling proposition? Does it sound a bit like a mission statement?

Good! It should. I do not know how many people would be interested in how to build a customer list and get clients. That sounds elementary to me, but who knows? They might want to subscribe to receive the weekly how-to articles though. We all need to know how to expand our Internet toolkit.

In your autoresponder you will have weekly articles or weekly links to articles on your blog. It is better to put the article in your blog and have the email refer to the blog. The email you send can have a short excerpt and a link to the article. Perhaps you add at the bottom of the email, "P.S. I found this great product that helped me double my sales, if you are interested in increasing your sales as well, check it out. Click here." The emails are all part of the overall picture. The people who read your great articles should be pleased and indeed interested in getting your newsletter. They appreciate receiving notifications of great how-to articles from you as you promised. You are offering real value. They will begin to anticipate an email from you. In addition to the great information, you always tell about some new product too. There is always some sort of an offer or a call to action. Your audience trusts you now and some will check it out and buy. Do you see how this all works together?

Follow these rules and you will have a great little resource box that is about the right size and acceptable to the majority of article marketing directory sites. Do you think people will actually click on a link and take a look at your website if you give them something for their effort like a white paper or free eBook? Yes. I think so.

VIRAL ARTICLE RECAP

When we're sitting at our desk and we're trying to decide what to write, where do we start? If we're talking about viral articles, it makes it even harder. In the case of a viral article, we want to get the article published and syndicated as many times as we can. What should we write about? We've gone into great depth in the chapters on endless content for our website. We know that when it comes to a viral article, we do not care about keeping our Bacon distance a couple steps away. We can make the distance as far as we want keeping in mind that if you can possibly stay on topic that is better. We want to write something that will go as viral as possible. It would be really cool if the article was re-published fifty or sixty times. That is hardly crazy viral, but it gives us fifty or sixty sites where our article has been published. These links are the most difficult to come by, but have the most worth as far as search engines are concerned. Article marketing the old fashioned way is still the best way to obtain these kinds of links. If you want to try to get other kinds of links, you will probably end up with reciprocal links which means you have to talk to somebody usually on the phone or through email. They will ask for a link on your site, you give them your link for their site. All links are great, but some are worth a lot more. For an authority site and for the kind of links and traffic we need, we want a one-way link back to us using a keyword phrase where we are the origination. This is the holy grail of all links.

BAD LINKS

I've talked a lot about what a great link is. Let's discuss the kind of links that can get you in trouble. *What Makes a Backlink Bad in the First Place?*

In case you are unsure, there are a variety of things that could cause a backlink to be considered "bad" or detrimental in the eyes of a search engine.

- Link networks. You can pay for links or join networks that were set up just to share links. You may have already seen these if you work with WordPress at all. A company creates a program that automatically adds comments to WordPress sites. That is one of the kinds of links that you can buy. We all know them as comment spam. This spam might last for a couple weeks before it is deleted. When you investigate your site to see if the links you paid for exist, you will find you have as many links as you purchased which could be hundreds. As soon as people start deleting these spam comments, our links are all gone and we've angered the search engines. Nobody gets a thousand links in a day like these services will give you. This is bad business and could do more harm than good. Stay as far away as you can.

- **Overly optimized links.** Having a keyword strategy is a good thing; it is probably how you started ranking in the first place. However, when your link is anchored from the same keyword, thousands of times, all over the Internet, search engine crawlers will probably suspect something is out of place. Varying your keyword strategy is critical. If you follow my advice and strategies, you will be just fine. I advise just enough, but not too much. Use keyword phrase blocks and let each article stand on its own merit. You do not need thirty articles using the same keyword phrase.

- **Links that just do not make sense.** If you have links living on sites that do not relate at all to your industry, or are across the world from your target audience, the search engine crawlers will notice. Links should be on relevant sites for best results.

- **Spam directory links.** If the directory exists for the sole purpose of building links and is completely unrelated to your business or niche, you should probably get out of there.

- **Duplicate content with links.** Guest posting can be a great way to increase your brand's exposure and to spread a link or two around the Internet. Sending the same content to multiple sites takes away from the practice. Instead of crafting one article and hoping multiple sites pick up on it (press releases, anyone?), pitch individual stories and posts to different sites. Use your links, but vary your content.

THIN CONTENT

Thin content is a relatively common problem. When you are only concerned with quantity, you can easily end up ignoring quality. If you ignore quality, Google will ignore you.

Some good examples of thin content are rogue content uploaded to a website without context. Basically, it is just content that has no substance and may not even make sense to a human reader. It is the kind of content that some of these "spinner" software programs create. Another example is pages with embedded videos with usually less than two paragraphs taken from third-party websites. Another is quick updates revolving around one or two paragraphs of content that do not provide value to readers. All three of these are basically the same thing. It is junk thrown together essentially just to make use of some keyword phrases. The content itself is near worthless. Google is not a fan of these practices. All unorthodox strategies revolving around thin content can backfire. The best course of action if you want to be safe and stay out of Google's crosshairs is and will always be to provide real content with enough words to make the article worthwhile. A good rule is to ask yourself if the article imparting some kind of valuable knowledge about the topic? This is not rocket science. It is common sense. Stay away from the tricks and short cuts and you will be fine.

Here are some other things that will get you in trouble. Stay away from creating true duplicates on your own website. Copies of your own pages within your website or across multiple domains will only make your content thinner. Moreover, duplicates can aggravate other existing thin content issues. Get rid of them as soon as possible. Stay away from near duplicates as well. Near duplicates refer to pages that vary by a negligible amount of web content, usually by not more than a couple lines. Maybe you are selling the same widget in multiple colors and sizes. You think it may be a good idea to promote your products using the same copy and changing only the words related to the color and size of every single item available. Perhaps you own a company providing services in different cities. You think it may be wise to save some time and energy by copy-pasting your content within your website on different pages while only changing the cities, keywords and headline. This used to be a reasonable strategy, but not anymore.

What about what is called "low unique ratio"? Some websites promote a small amount of unique content and use complex navigation and dynamic content to mask this flaw. If ninety-eight percent of your page is just structure and the rest is content that is supposed to inform, educate and entertain your readers, you've got problems. Maybe you have what Google calls "high ad ratio". Traffic exchanges and other advertising sites may be great money making sites, but with Google changing the way they rate your sites, you are on your own in getting traffic if you own one of these sites. Now what? Your clever strategy is exposing you to a series of Google penalties simply because your website is jam-packed with lots and lots of ad banners. A "too-high ad ratio" is linked to an insufficient amount of content.

GARBAGE ON THE INTERNET?

Let's face it; the Internet is stuffed with garbage. Google is trying to fix it. They are trying to rank websites according to their truthfulness. Google's search engine currently uses the number of incoming links to a web page as a proxy for quality, determining where it appears in search results. This is what this book has been instructing you to do. I'm instructing you to create valid links that demonstrate *Web Authority* and value without trying every black hat trick in the book. In Google's eyes, pages with many links from other sites rank higher. It stands to reason that if many other webmasters link to you because you provide a service for these webmasters or are the best information for a particular subject, you should rank higher. This system has brought us the search engine as we know it today. The downside is that websites full of misinformation can mess up the rankings if enough people link to them. The fix that Google is implementing makes the strategies in this book even more valuable. Websites that abuse their privileges will be going away. Follow the rules and you stand a much better ability to rank even higher.

A Google research team is adapting a model to measure the trustworthiness of a page, rather than its reputation on the web. Instead of just counting incoming links, the system which is not yet live as of the writing of this book, counts the number of incorrect facts within a page as well. The idea is that a website with content that has few false facts is considered to be trustworthy. The score they will compute for each page will be called its "Knowledge-Based Trust score." This new strategy works by tapping into the "Knowledge Vault". The knowledge vault is a vast store of facts that Google has pulled off the Internet. These are facts the web unanimously agrees are considered truth. Web pages that contain contradictory information are bumped down the rankings. Whether we like it or not, as webmasters, we're going to be expected to provide real value to our readers. For those of us that are honest and want to provide real value, finally we will be getting the recognition we deserve. Finally the cheaters will get what they deserve. It is about time.

WRITING STUFF

Yes, we do have to write stuff. It is the nature of the beast. If you want to create your own *Web Authority* and in so doing, sell a lot of product, you have to write stuff. The reason becomes more obvious when you remember the Internet is just a lot of words and patterns of words. As we have seen, it is important to provide that visually pleasing experience to our readers along with valuable content. But what about the search engines of the world? A search engine, as far as we're concerned, is some software that visits our website trying to rank us and index our website so people can find it. We have to keep both happy. In a nutshell, if that is the entire Internet consists of, words and patterns of words then it would stand to reason that content is indeed king and we have to write stuff. We have to provide content to the search engines. Content is the food that a search engine desires and devours.

What about us and our desires? We're trying to build traffic for your sites so you can sell lots of product. We have to give the search engines what they want in order to be rewarded with that traffic. You do not have to do any of this if you do not want to. There is an alternative. You can pay for all your traffic. If you have a lot of money that you can blow on paid advertising, that is fine, go for it. I'm talking about free traffic provided by the search engines.

One of the nice things about free traffic is that your website works all on its own and you don't have to feed it money. I'm not saying you won't be doing any advertising at all, but whatever percentage of traffic you can create from the methods this book teaches is money you save.

CONTENT SOURCES

In this section of the book we are going to discuss where we can find content if we hate to write stuff ourselves. There are a variety of different sources. We will discuss those sources and typical prices and then we will talk about managing the process.

Where do you get content? The first place is obvious, you could do it yourself. Another resource might be to get together with some friends. If you have some people you work with on the Internet, you can get a group together towards a common goal. I find that Skype or another instant messenger service is a great place to find like-minded friends. If you are not out on Skype, you should be. You can and should be part of my team and my group.

Stop right now, go to your computer, and add me as a contact on Skype. If you do not have Skype, you can download it at http://www.skype.com. Once installed, use the "Add Contacts" menu item, type 'Salesnav' and ask to be a contact of mine. Ask me to add you to our "Doc's Internet Funnel Group". If you are trying to create and run an online home-based business, it is extremely difficult to do this all on your own. You need friends. You do not have to participate or feel like you have to answer every little question that someone might ask, but at least you learn what is going on every day and keep abreast of new developments, tools, events, etc. In my group there are five or six different kinds of webcasts and events going on every single day. You will become part of the online community and start meeting people. After a while, you will recognize some of the same names at different events and webinars. You will know who is consistent, who is going to stick around, who is serious, and who is not. You will learn who has something that they can offer you and, hopefully, you have something to offer them. That is the way it works.

Most of these people are working for themselves from their homes. Perhaps you are working on a project. There are some things that you do very well. There are some things that you do not. You see some things that others do well. For a good joint venture to work; everybody pieces each person's best talents together and it develops into a win-win for everyone. There are so many variations that it is really up to the individuals involved. Be creative.

Then we have general purpose outsourcing and crowd-sourcing. Whether you write the content yourself, or you have a group of people that help gather the content, or whether you spend a little bit of money here and there for content, the bottom line is that you are providing the content for your site that provides the traffic, the links, and the sales.

Why write the articles yourself if you do not have to? The reasons are simple. If you know how to write it isn't that hard for you and does not cost anything. If you cannot do the writing yourself, there are all kinds of resources to help you.

Find out about webinars done by a colleague Don Legere on Content Curation if you are still having trouble thinking up ideas for content. http://www.Internetsalesfunnel.com

One idea is Content Curation. Content curation solves a problem that is a constant issue on the Internet. There are already all kinds of content available. It depends on what topic you've chosen, but many times while searching for information on the internet you find articles that are outdated. The information is no longer correct or no longer applies. Things that were going on last year do not matter in many topics. Change, especially with technology, is accelerating; it is not slowing down. This gives you an advantage because if you keep your nose to the grindstone and find out what is going on, and you listen and learn, you might find yourself more knowledgeable about the topic than what is already published. That may be simply because you incorporated what is new. In as little as a year's time, you can be more knowledgeable than anybody else just from being more current.

What was going on last year might still apply, but not as much. Look at your telephone. Look at your cell phone. Look at the phones from last year. I have a three year old droid cellphone. It is almost embarrassing to let some of my friends see it, but it still does the job. With content curation, find articles that are dated and rewrite them and make them current. Make them your own.

By writing articles yourself, you get better and better at it over time. Practice makes perfect. It is not that hard to write a two hundred and fifty to five hundred word article on something if you just start writing it, but you might be one of those people that hate to write anything or your spelling or grammar is horrible. For some people, it is not easy at all and I do understand that. On the other hand, the more you practice, the better you are going to be. One advantage to writing at least some of the material yourself is that when you do build a team, you will know what good content versus bad content looks like and how long it takes to write. You will be better at managing your team. You will know how long it should take, especially if somebody is charging you.

When you are writing by yourself, you will have a relatively small volume. All I'm asking you to do manage a minimum of one article a week. If you can write more than that, that is wonderful. Trying to write ten to fifteen articles in one day is crazy, but I know people that have done that just to jump-start their site. The more articles you write, the more traffic you get.

Once you meet some Internet marketing friends, find a niche you want to work on together, and decide on a financial arrangement that makes sense for everybody, you might start what I would call your "in-house" team. In order to provide large quantities of content, people are building in-house teams. What is an in-house team if you are home alone? I'm not talking about having a collection of computers at your house and having to feed everybody lunch every day. I mean maybe five or six people widely distributed across the entire world, all assisting each other to get something done. An in-house team is not actually in-house employees; they are virtual contractors of sorts.

Again, a tool like Skype or some other instant messenger will keep all of you in constant contact. Writing is a widely available skill. If you know how to write, it should not be difficult to quantify or qualify the skills of the people in your team. With the Internet and an instant messenger, it should be easy to manage everyone.

Content is a must for a site owner and more so than ever before. Google will penalize you if you try to take shortcuts. You must be consistently writing content. You have to keep it up. You cannot stop. Blogs are news based and use RSS (Really Simple Syndication) feeds. That means old news isn't worth indexing. In fact, Google may forget you in just over one week. Over a period of time, if you stop, you may stop getting traffic altogether - at least from the Google blog search engine. All you have to do is your minimum one article a week to stay indexed in both types of search engines. Content on your blog is one of those animals that you continually have to feed. It is now part of your life online. It is also an advantage for you because most people get started, put in a lot of time, get all excited, go for it, get tired, and quit. It creates opportunity for those that stick with it. The bottom line is that if you stop adding content, if you stand still for even a little while, you are falling behind.

One of the things about content is that it is highly scalable. You can ramp up any way you want and as fast as you want. There are places that you can go to get content. They are called article services and writing brokers. Do a search. Type "article services" or "writing brokers" in a Google search window. There are too many to list. By the way, if you are a prolific writer yourself, maybe you would like to become a contributor for, or even start your own article service or brokerage. There are lots of ways to make money on the Internet. The need for original material is going to become even more important over the next few years as we've seen. These services vary in price and quality. You will find the two as different business models. An article service is usually one person and it's the same person that writes the articles. A writing broker is one person that you talk to, but that person represents many writers.

Article services and writing brokers can be an easy and fast solution to bring you content. There will be some management on your part of these services, but you usually have only one contact at each of these types of services. If you have a consistent or recurrent need, such as one article every week on a particular subject, you might be able to work something out with someone and never have to write your own articles.

Let's take a look at some of the differences between an article service and a brokerage. An article service is a single source while writing brokers are more of a clearing house. Both have somebody else who is writing articles for you. For the brokerage, there may be several or many people involved, but you only have one person you talk to. A broker manages your wants and needs and is somebody who handles all of that for you.

An article service contact is usually the same person as the writer. Managing your own article service writers individually is simple on a small scale. As you grow, you may want to move to a broker. Brokers manage those relationships and support for you. On the other hand brokers sometimes have a limited assurance of quality because there are a lot of people writing and quality can have lots of variations.

Every type of article service or brokerage is going to be slightly different and so the quality is going to be slightly different. Just realize that these services are out there and available and there is lots of them and they can be very reasonable.

SOME CONTENT ARTICLE SERVICES AND BROKERAGES

NeedAnArticle.com

TextBroker.com

TheContentAuthority.com

MyWriters.com

If you do a lot of writing and enjoy it, I encourage you to take a look at some of these sites and see exactly what they are doing. They have a business model. It may not be your thing, but you might consider starting your own writing company or becoming a contributor for extra money. By the way, these were good sites as of the writing of this book, but things change. Check the sites out on someplace like Alexa.com for an overall ranking. Rate the different sites. Take a look and see how much traffic some of these sites and their articles are getting. Note whether or not they are publishing their own articles. Where are they publishing their own articles? Are you getting an original article? Do you have to maintain links back to different places and are there any other unusual contract requirements?

GENERAL PURPOSE OUTSOURCING

General purpose outsourcing is the practice of hiring someone to write the article for you on a general outsourcing website. Basically, you hire people to write your articles, but they are not from a content service. Three I use are Elance.com, Odesk.com and Fiverr.com. I use Elance.com and Fiverr.com often.

On services like Elance.com and Odesk.com, you can quantify what you want and take bids. After bidding, you accept the worker, pay a deposit, and when the work is completed, pay them. You do have to be very careful, but you can get almost anything done you want. The problem is that you never know what kind of quality you will get. My experiences so far have been pretty good. The bottom line is that there are many people in the world online that can afford to work for a lot less. There are people from all over the world offering their abilities and talents. Some of those people are extremely good at what they do. You have to decide for yourself if it is better to hire someone for a lot less or use your own time. I find at times that my time is better spent on other projects and it makes total sense for me to hire someone.

Fiverr is another site you may be familiar with. It is five dollars for just about anything you want like someone to write an article. You could spend five bucks dollars a week, or about twenty dollars a month and you would be stocking your site well. The only thing I caution you on is keeping the quality within your own expectations and keeping the search engines happy.

There is also one other content source you can use and it is called crowd-sourcing. It utilizes nameless, faceless workers. It is a de-personalized workforce. You might not ever even know who wrote your article. I'm talking about MTurk.com. It is called Amazon

Mechanical Turk. It is named for a late 1700s hoax. Someone built a mechanical chess-playing machine. The hoax was that there was really a person in the machine. Amazon created a marketplace where "turkers" perform human intelligence tasks which are called HITS. It has been a real innovation for outsourcing. There are some entire businesses based on providing HITS to others. Whether you become a Turker yourself or you just use the services, you can get just about anything done on Mturk.com. The last time I looked, there were 193,000 different jobs or HITS available. Not only can this be a resource, but it is also a place where you can offer your own services.

MTurk.com is a random sample of humanity. The return on your investment can be fantastic when it is done right. For example, two-hundred and fifty words can cost as little as a dollar. On the other hand, you may have to edit it because the writer's English may not be up to par. Turkers are real humans, not artificial intelligence, and they come from all over the world. It is a fantastic place to get text translated for next to nothing though. Very small tasks are always best. The smaller the task, the easier it is to get good quality back. Strangely, getting an article written is a perfect kind of task.

Writing an HIT is not as easy as you think. You have to be specific and really detail what you want or you will not get what you ask for. Pricing what you will pay is an art form and it takes a little bit of time to get used to it. Things that drive costs are the article length, the content quality, the management, the support, and whether you want guarantees. Caveat emptor means buyer beware. A common price for full articles will give you an idea of what you should or should not be paying. Six, ten, or thirteen US dollars is about right for two-hundred and fifty to one thousand words. This is comparable to Fiverr.com. A blog sized post should be two to five dollars. That gives you roughly two hundred to five hundred words. Just be careful. Ten dollars is not always better than six dollars. It really depends on the person doing the work.

HAVING A CONTENT PIPELINE

Let's talk about your "Content Pipeline". First, you actually have to have one. You cannot have three articles a year and expect to get any kind of traffic out of it. You will get some small amount of traffic, but blogs are news-based and you have to provide new news. It works like this. Two articles, one written today and one written six months ago, are exactly the same. The one that just got written will get most of the traffic. I'm suggesting a modest one article a week. Do not stand still because that is falling behind. Using my techniques, you can give your articles more longevity on the regular Google search engine side, but standing still means Google's blog search will forget you altogether.

A content pipeline might look like this. You have already written all your product articles with payment buttons. You only add more product pages if you add more products to your items you sell. You choose twelve to fifteen keyword phrases related to your topic. Over the next twelve to fifteen weeks, you write one information article a week. The next week will be a viral article to be published. Continue providing one article a week, product, informational, or viral.

If you do not have a content pipeline, you can bet your competitor does. You have to add some content at some rate every month. Content is, ultimately, your source of traffic, so treat it accordingly. **Doc Stone Tip:** *Your web business is partly a publishing business.* The Internet is just a collection of words and phrases. Give it what it wants. It wants content. I should come up with a t-shirt that says, "Feed the Beast." Manage your content. Have a content strategy.

WHERE I GET MY CONTENT IDEAS

Doc Stone Tip: The only way for me to be knowledgeable enough to talk to anyone else is to get information from as many places as I can. So, when something grabs my attention, I sign up for it so that I get emails. I put all the emails into folders for the different topics. When I'm looking for something to write, I will go through the folders and find something that looks interesting. I study it, add to it, make it my own, and update the content. If it is something that the original author should get credit for, I acknowledge it. We can all learn from someone else. We are all always borrowing and rewording what we've heard from various sources and giving our opinions. Put it in your own words. That way, you will thoroughly understand what you are writing. That is where I come up with a lot of my material. I have a pile of information that I look through to find something to write about.

LET'S RECAP

We've been talking about how my brand of *Web Authority* article marketing can bring in a significant amount of free targeted traffic to your website. I've outlined for you three types of articles and how they are used together on article marketing sites and your own blog to achieve these results. I've told you that all traffic comes from content and links. Because of that, all traffic and traffic problems can be solved with more good content on and off-site. Onsite means on your blog. Offsite means syndicated and re-published. We've said content is king and links are queen. We discussed different ways to achieve all this. We discussed how to widen your syndication and get links for next to nothing - the best way to get links. If you can get something published and it is viral enough, the links will grow plenty. The more links you have, the more traffic you have, the higher the page ranking. The higher your page ranking, the more traffic you get. It is kind of a two-edged sword and both must be accomplished. The more you do, the more you get. The better you are, the more you get. You are rewarded with more traffic for picking up more traffic and more links. The end result is an Authority site.

SOME MISTAKES AND MISCONCEPTIONS

You have to have some kind of strategy otherwise you will see mixed results. You may find that some days, you write great material. Other days, it is not so great. Content creation has to be one of your main tasks every week and the writing needs to be consistent. There are a few things to avoid doing if you do not want to develop bad content. If you concentrate on creating great content and avoiding some of these pitfalls, most of what you write will be quite good. Here's a list of some things to avoid.

1. <u>Writing Only When the Mood Takes You</u>. You can't sit around waiting for your mood to show up on command. Waiting for inspiration can take days, months, or even years. You should be aiming for on-time delivery of content. Schedule time to write. Write every day, even if you do not want to. The more you practice, the better it gets.

2. <u>Going Big or Going Home</u>. Very few of us are ever going to achieve greatness. **Doc Stone tip:** Quality is very important, but greatness is not. We all aspire to be great and over time and you just might achieve it, but do not lose sight of the objective. Most of us just want to make sales of our product and make a living, not become Charles Dickens. Do the best you can. Over time, you will get better and better and that is quite alright.

3. <u>Writing for Yourself First</u>: Writing for yourself means forgetting your target audience and writing something you like, but not necessarily what your particular readers want to read. Again, our objective is to make sales by providing the right kind of content. Writing for yourself does not achieve your objective. It is okay if you love to write, but save those for another blog.

4. <u>Backwards Article Marketing</u>. There are two ways to use an article marketing directory site. You can be the author or you can use someone else's articles. Google has caught on and removed using someone else's articles as a valid way to drive people to your site. That means that you have to be the one writing the articles, not using them from other authors. Today, back linking is used as a method of determining the legitimacy of a site and how well connected it is with its peers. To that end, re-publishing articles garnered from other authors or article marketing sites is almost certain to produce few results. While it may not be the best practice, it is still very widespread and that is good for us. As long as webmasters are either lazy or unable to produce their own content, or maybe they have built in traffic and don't need to advertise, re-publishing will never go away. It is just that we won't be the ones who re-publish.

5. <u>Bypassing Blogging and Going to Social Media</u>. Some bloggers get most of their visits from Facebook, Twitter, and other social media. That is great, but as I've been saying, a blog is a unique vehicle like

no other for attracting organic search traffic. Add plugins to tie your blog to your Facebook and Twitter accounts. When you write your articles and post, they post to both. Comments on one appear on the other and vice-versa. Social media is a wonderful tool and one you should make great use of, but why would you want to eliminate such an important tool as Google search engines and depend on just social media? In addition, Facebook's terms of use clearly state that content that is produced and put on their site is theirs under copyright. **Doc Stone Tip:** Do not give up your ownership.

6. <u>Doing it All Yourself, All the Time</u>. As you grow, you just might need some help. I've spent an entire chapter on how to find content sources for very few dollars. You might be able to do well at first, but as the sales increase and the day-to-day grind of the business gets in the way of your creativity, the first thing to suffer is your writing. You will know it when it happens. Do not slow down. Please get some help.

7. <u>Writing Once a Month</u>. Although you do not have to write an article once a day, you should write more than once a month. Multiple times a week is preferable, but once a week is the minimum. Also, you may lose the interest of your readers by taking too long to add content to your blog. That will cost you traffic. But mostly, it is to keep the search engines coming back to index another page as often as possible that is important.

PITFALLS TO AVOID

Mediocre content has no place on your blog. Stay away from these mistakes. Do not be willing to sacrifice the reputation of your blog.

1. <u>Bad Optimization</u>. We've been discussing at length exactly how to do proper SEO work on each article and page you create. The key is to do enough, but not too much. No black hat practices are necessary.

2. <u>Bad Formatting.</u> Try and organize and prioritize your ideas to be coherent. You may be the smartest person on the face of the earth, but your readers are not. Do not talk down to them or treat them

like children either. Try and stay as middle of the road as you can. Make sure you explain everything or create links to explanations for things you think might not be understood. Use paragraph breaks to denote separate thoughts or concepts. **Doc Stone Tip:** Remember this rule. Keep your concepts to three things you want your readers to remember. Tell them what you are going to tell them, detail each item, and then tell them what you told them. Use bullet points to organize your ideas more effectively. Transform large chunks of text into smaller paragraphs. The search engines won't care about your formatting, but your readers will.

3. Bad Audience Tone Who is your audience? What kind of person do you think will read what you have written? Do you know who you are talking to? Research and analyze your targeted audience (age, gender, shopping behavior, preferences and concerns and so on). A lot depends on the products and the topic, but the closer you get to your audience, the better.

4. Too Much Ad Content. You are trying to sell stuff, yes, but be subtle. Do not hit people over the head with "Buy this, buy this, and buy this! Too much Google AdSense may come with penalties, too. Creating too much "salesy" content is a counterproductive approach. It will deter your visitors and make you seem money-hungry.

5. Bad Scheduling. *Once a week minimum!* Forgetting to blog at least every week will get you penalized by Google simply because you don't produce content. Google hates an on/off schedule, but will eat up a regular content flow. Try it. Stop for a while and see what happens to your traffic.

6. Yawn-Inspiring Content. Is your content boring and uninspired? Expand your knowledge. Dig a little deeper and put some effort into it. Once of the reasons I try to get people to pick a topic they enjoy is so they do not get bored writing about it. If you are bored, how in the world will you inspire anyone?

7. Duplicate Content. Duplicate content is forbidden. It comes with penalties from search engines. Do not do it. While content curation and borrowing someone else's idea is ok, you have to make them

your own. Besides, a lot of your readers will recognize plagiarism at a first glance.

8. Irrelevant, Useless Web Writing. If your content does not improve the lives of your readers at least on some level, think twice before crafting or distributing it.

9. Web Writing Services Provided by a Friend of a Friend. I've given you a number of places that you can hire folks who will do a good job with your content for very little. Ultimately though, you are the final judge of what goes on your site. The kid down the street that is still in high school writing your articles for a dollar each may sound like a good idea, but read it first, then decide.

10. Expert Advice Provided by a Clueless Person. While I am writing this book, I am well aware that not all of my ideas are unique. I heard some of them from someone else. I did have to put two and two together and come up with my own ideas. The art of article marketing is nothing new, but the way I have described it updates it in today's world and the ideas are definitely new and innovative. Article marketing the way they taught five years ago is somewhat black hat and will not work these days. I've not heard anyone else grasp what I have, actually put it in practice, and make it work. It took me a long time to figure it out by practice, trial and error. Take the time to research each item you write about. You do not want to be called on the carpet or embarrassed someday for something you were clearly wrong about. That being said, you do have to be bold enough to walk and talk like an expert. Most of your readers land on your page to look for facts, not fiction. To avoid public embarrassment and credibility issues, do your homework before writing your articles.

11. The Dangerous "Me Too" Approach. Let's say your product is basically the same exact thing that four thousand affiliates all have too. What makes you different? If you cannot separate and articulate what it is about doing business with you versus your competitors, buyers won't have a legitimate reason to respond to your calls to action.

12. Empty Content. Empty or thin content is that fourth category of article we do not want on our sites. It is called junk. Pages like an

FAQ whose sole purpose is to link other pages will bring you nothing but trouble from search engines.

13. Redundant, Overlapping Content. Creating variations of articles or "spinning" just for the purpose of covering a block of keyword phrases does not work anymore. If you use a spinner program to spin many versions of the same article, expect penalties from the search engines. That is duplicate content you tried to hide. Make sure you always deliver user-oriented, information-rich, SEO-friendly content that can be digested by your readers.

14. Content without Calls-to-Action. Tell your readers what to do! Ask them to read the rest of your articles, subscribe to your newsletter, or try your new product. Do not assume they even see the autoresponder on the sidebar of the blog. Yes, it is obvious to me and you, but a busy page and what human brains miss sometimes can be amazing. Do not leave it to chance. Do not be bossy either; just suggest a next course of action.

15. Auto Generated Content. This is so foolish. Letting a machine generate your content is like a death sentence. Using services that provide you content without reviewing the article first is also foolish. If it is good content, great, use it, but do not trust anyone but you. On top of that, these services provide the same article to all their clients. It is all duplication.

16. Grammatically Incorrect Content. Not all readers are concerned about grammar and it happens even on the best sites. Use the tools available for your editor. The biggest problem is that too many mistakes makes you look like you do not care. If you do not care, why should your reader? The products must be mediocre too.

17. Offensive Content. Using offensive content when you are trying to sell product is like insulting your buyers. Use good judgment, common sense, and politeness. Stay neutral or do not bother. Point out both sides if necessary for your topic of choice, but do not take sides.

18. Unorganized Content. Use the blog the way it is meant to be used. Create categories, menus, and whatever else you have to do to make navigation on your site easy and enjoyable.

19. <u>Ancient-Looking Content.</u> Include a graphic if you can and try and stay away from text only content. If you can add video, webinar recordings, podcasts, infographics, charts and audio you will bring your blog back to life.

20. <u>Un-shareable Content.</u> It is so easy to add social buttons to all your articles with a single plugin. Make it easy for people to share your content and make comments.

21. <u>Taboo Topics.</u> If you are selling products, stay away from taboo subjects that will offend half your target market just because of something they perceive you to believe. Topics such as religion, racism, and politics have no business on your blog.

22. <u>Negativity Everywhere.</u> You should always reflect that your company is excellent, your products are flawless, and your customers are happy. Maintain good vibes. Give people something to smile about and share the good word about your business.

23. <u>Proofread!</u> Reread what you've written. Does it make sense? Check the spelling. Check the grammar. Double check those important words that resonate with your brand and image. It will be worth it. I went through this book three times and had 5 editors help me proofread it. It took almost as long to edit than it did to write.

HOW TO GET NOTICED

Build your story. Readers shouldn't have to wonder who you are. Build your brand recognition. That is you. Use your name or a pen name and build the name. Make sure your profile, author photo, areas of expertise, goals and past achievements are somewhere on your site. Maintain links to your Facebook, Twitter, and Linked In pages. Focus on your strengths. You may have expertise in multiple fields. That is great, but stay focused. Being great at woodworking isn't something to mention in your bio when the site is all about software. Get the essentials right. **Doc Stone Tip: S**top focusing on traffic and getting sales and concentrate on creating a connection with the reader. That is your first job. You are creating informational articles to bring readers to your site hoping that they might be interested in buying something, but if you cannot make a connection first, you won't get any further. Act like a professional. If you walk into an appliance store and some guy with bad breath comes up to you and starts acting like he is some kind of appliance genius, you will be turned off. But if that same guy brushed his teeth, wore nice clothes, and acted professional, you would be much more likely to trust him and buy something. It is basic human nature. We may be doing all of our business online, but this truth still is in effect. Your personality, attitude, and ability to communicate professionally should be at the top of your list to improve.

Perfect your timing. Timing is everything. When we discussed certain topics to write about, many of them were very time sensitive. Stay abreast of new developments in your industry or with your topic. Readers will recognize you as the one that provides a service to them. They will learn to know, like, and trust you because of it. Make everything user-friendly. Make every part of your business easy to use. Your readers should be able to understand and follow everything they see. Embrace change with confidence. I've been in some kind of management role my whole life. When I start managing a new company, my goal is to weed out all the people that hate change. My goal is to make it so people are excited about what is going to happen today. People get so comfortable with their routine; they forget that change is part of business. In fact, I believe that staying the same in business, doing things the way we always have, can be a death sentence. Sometimes those changes may affect you negatively. That is ok, mistakes happen. Evolve and embrace change. Be prepared for change. It can come from any direction at any time. Change can also become opportunity.

Praise your competition. First, know who your competition is and what they do. It does you no good to bad mouth them. Rather, articulate why you can provide better service, more support, easier installation, or whatever you can to stand alone above your competition. There is no need for negativity. In the world of Internet marketing, most people work from home. You might hear from your competition and end up working together on a project. Keep your options open. Finally, thank your readers. Offer something to your readers for free and thank them for participating. Always give them more than they paid for.

ARTICLE CONSTRUCTION AND SEO

     Now it is time to talk about search engines and reveal my blog SEO secrets for achieving *Web Authority*. We've already touched on this quite a bit. Some search engines and SEO websites out there purport to give you all the information you need to make an intelligent choice of keyword phrases. The problem is figuring out what to write about. Using keyword tools is something you want yourself to become much more proficient using and interpreting. What keyword phrases will bring the most return for your efforts? Most of these tools work the same way. Enter a basic idea and the software will return a list of related keyword phrases and give you some idea of the amount of traffic one might expect. At best, most only give you a rough idea of the traffic and analytics for each keyword phrase. You have to know how to interpret the results. There can be a lot of pitfalls. Here is an example of the keyword phrase "weight-loss plan". Google used to have a great free tool, but now it is buried in Google AdWords. You have to have an account to use it, but you do not have to spend any money if you do not want to. It is still the closest to accurate. Some of the information returned can be confusing. In terms of competition, you only get high, medium, or low. They tell you the high, medium, and low in terms of AdWords, not general searches. Still, it is a good indication of how many people are fighting over the use of a particular keyword. Google defines competition as it relates to AdWords as:

Competition: The number of advertisers that showed on each keyword relative to all keywords across Google. Note that this data is specific to the location and Search Network targeting that you've selected. In the "Competition" column, you can see whether the competition for a keyword is low, medium, or high.

In other words, how many people are trying to use that keyword phrase or paying for that keyword phrase? High, medium, and low involves all of the categories of possible paid advertising including cell phones, tablets, desktop computers, partner sites, and Google AdSense. It includes every form of advertising or add-on that Google tracks or allows you to have. High competition means that you have a very small chance of getting anywhere near the top. Not only are people using that keyword phrase a lot, they are also paying big money for that keyword phrase. Medium just means there is not as many. Google hasn't said what the difference between low and high, and high and medium, where they start and stop, and how many searches it is. Competition has nothing to do with the number of searches for a phrase; it has to do with how many people are competing for a particular keyword phrase.

Google also shows you general searches with a number that is split into global searches and local searches. What is the cutoff between global and local? It turns out it depends on what you have defined as local. Check your settings. Your settings should reflect your physical location or what part of the world you want to target.

WHO IS YOUR COMPETITION?

We touched on this earlier. It's easy to think of your competition in the traditional sense, but this is the Internet. Everybody thinks their competition is the store down the street that has the same product or maybe a website with the same or similar products with a cheaper price. That assumption is true to a certain extent, but actually, not at all when it comes to the Internet. If you are selling widget number one out of your home, and you live out in the middle of nowhere, and there are four local stores in town selling widget number one, and they are all competing for a limited market, but none of them have a website, you really do not have any competition, do you? That is because your main competition really is the next website using your same keyword phrases and doing a better job at it than you are. If the next website online is doing a bad job of search engine optimization on their site, then it is like having a store in town with the lights off at night while they are still supposedly open. Your competition is websites using the same keyword phrases that you are trying to rank for that is on page one of Google. Your job is to do a better job ranking than they are. Your job is to turn the lights up brighter than the competition. You are never going to get all available traffic for the keyword phrase because page one always has at least eight to ten websites listed, but if you can get even a significant portion of that traffic, it would certainly help. People searching for something online rarely check past page three. You need to rank on page one or two at minimum for as many keyword phrases for your topic as you can. The more articles that you write for blocks of particular keyword phrases, the brighter the lights.

HOW TO FIND KEYWORD PHRASES WITHOUT SO MUCH COMPETITION

What kind of angle should you use? There are quite a few keyword tools out there. Do not rely on the direct approach so much. Go indirect in your thinking. Remember the dog leash example? The easy and simple keyword phrase one would think should be the keyword phrase "dog leash". What you will find is that the competition is very stiff for those two words with people spending tons on advertising. For the small online business, you cannot possibly compete. So do not bother. There is a lot wrong with choosing 'dog leash' anyway. One, there are not enough words in the phrase. Two, you are going to have an incredible amount of competition. Three, the two words 'dog leash' are also included in every keyword phrase of any length that also includes those two words in that order. Think about dog leashes indirectly, off to the side. What problems does a dog leash solve? As you are doing your research on keyword phrases, you are looking for what problems dog leashes solve. You will start finding keyword phrases that have escaped everybody else that have may have quite a bit of traffic. After doing research, you find your competition hasn't actually used that phrase properly for their SEO or they have only just happened to use the phrase in the body of the article or page. If you do just a little bit better on the SEO work, over time, you will start receiving some of that traffic. Jump on it. Go write the article. There is so much I could write about doing search engine optimization, that I could devote another entire book on it and never finish all my thoughts. This work is giving you the basics on writing the article so that you make best use of your keyword phrases.

What we're going to discuss now is how to find that keyword phrase and how to write the article. First, determine your market. You are in a global market now. If you are selling items that you are shipping within the United States, but really cannot be shipped overseas or even across state lines, perhaps you need to concentrate on your local market and not worry so much about the global market. If you plan on selling only within the town and surrounding areas where you live, it is a totally different strategy. You do not have quite the competition in a local market. If you have a typical advertising product, or some kind of software, or a plugin, or training system, you may be only selling in English speaking countries. If you are selling that kind of a product, then you may have a global market. For physical items that you might ship or have drop shipped, maybe your market is your local country. Is that a big enough market? Yes, it is a huge market unless you are on an island somewhere. Understand what your market is and exactly who you are targeting. You have to know where to aim if you are going to hit the target, right?

So you found some keyword phrases you think will work. You work with the Google AdWords keyword tool or some other keyword tool and review the results. You want to find a phrase that has low competition and a fair amount of traffic. I encourage the indirect thinking in finding your keyword phrases because you almost always have much less competition. I also encourage four, five, or even as many as eight word keyword phrases. You have a much better chance of scoring the traffic available.

A step left out by most everybody is next. Time to do our own research and not rely on what the particular keyword tool we used told us. Open a browser, enter each keyword phrase and take a look yourself. There are a lot of reasons for this. Take a look at the top websites on page one. You have to determine why they made page one in order for you to get to page one. Browsers support the ability to right click and select "View Page Source". You need to find the Meta tags for title, description, and keyword phrases. What keyword phrase were they trying to rank for? Many times, you will find it is not the one you thought. Nobody will ever know exactly what Google's algorithm actually is. There are 'experts' that will tell you what Google is thinking, but they do not really know for sure unless they are part of the team that wrote the code. Google's algorithm is always changing anyway. We have to make our own assumptions. It turns out most of this is common sense. Since the Internet is all words and phrases, let's keep this very basic.

All we want to do is be slightly better at doing our search engine optimization than the competition. Never overdo it. We want to only do just one phrase better than your competition. I will show you what that means.

BASIC SEARCH ENGINE OPTIMIZATION

The following is a short compilation of different aspects of a typical webpage and how a search engine like Google views each characteristic. It is not exhaustive, but should give you enough to understand the basics.

Keyword use in document title: The title is the text within the <title>...</title> tags in the HTML code of your web page.

Example: <title>Your web page title</title>

Global link popularity of web site: The global link popularity measures how many web pages link to your site. The number of web pages linking to your site is not as important as the quality of the web pages that link to your site. All major search engines take the quality and the context of the links into account. Search engines assume that your web page must offer relevant content if many quality sites link to it.

Link texts of inbound links: Inbound links are links from other web sites to your site. If many other sites link to your site, then Search Engines consider your site to be important. However, the number of links is not as important as is the relevance of the linking page and the link text used in linking to your site.

Keyword use in body text: The body text is the text on your web page that can be seen by people in their web browsers. It does not include HTML commands, comments, etc. The more visible text there is on a web page, the more a search engine can index. The calculations include spaces and punctuation marks.

Age of web site: Spam sites often come and go quickly. For this reason, search engines tend to trust a web site that has been around for a long time over one that is brand new. The age of the domain is seen as a sign of trustworthiness because it cannot be faked. The data is provided by Alexa.com (or Archive.org if Alexa.com does not have data about a site).

Keyword use in H1 headline texts: H1 headline texts are the texts that are written between the <h1>...</h1> tags in the HTML code of a web page. Some search engines give extra relevance to search terms that appear in the headline texts. This chapter examines if this applies to Google.com (without Places), too.

Example: <h1>your very big headline text</h1>

Keyword use in domain name: The domain name is the main part of the web page address. Google.com (without Places) gives extra relevance to search terms within the domain name. In the past, this was a major factor. If you sold light bulbs and owned lightbulbs.com, you would never have to advertise your website.

Example: "your-keyword" is the domain name of http://www.your-keyword.com

Keyword use in page URL: The page URL is the part after the domain name in the web page address. Google.com (without Places) gives extra relevance to search terms within the page URL. Separate your search terms in the page URL with slashes, dashes or underscores.

Example: "keyword/another-keyword.htm" is the page URL of http://www.domain.com/keyword/another-keyword.htm

Links from social networks: On social network sites, people decide which web sites are popular. This means that the popularity on social network sites cannot be easily influenced. For this reason, search engines might trust web sites more if they are popular on social networks.

Other factors such as server speed, use of your keyword phrase in H2 to H6 headline texts, and use of the phrase in an IMG ALT attribute matter. Bolding a keyword phrase in the body of the article, overall traffic, keyword use in same domain link texts also matter.

This is just a small sample of the most important aspects of optimizing a webpage for search engines.

REAL WORLD EXAMPLE

Let's take our 'weight-loss plan' example and see some results. According to the keyword tool I used at the time, 'weight-loss plan' has high competition. It has 368,000 searches globally and 201,000 searches locally. Locally in this case is just California. What most people think is, "Oh my, that is wonderful. That is a lot of searches? If I could just get a couple per cent of that traffic every month, it would be awesome." There is a problem with that, though. If you look at the keyword phrases in the list returned by the keyword tool, 'weight-loss plan' is included in almost every single one of them. What does that mean? It means that the 368,000 includes every other keyword phrase that it is used in. Above it, we see 'best weight-loss plan'. "Best weight-loss plan" is 22,000 searches of the 368,000. We also see 'quick weight-loss plans'. That is 14,000 of the 368,000. The bottom line is that one must assume that 'weight-loss plan' is not a good keyword phrase to use. Is this true? Maybe, we'd have to check it in a browser and view some of the source code on each site to really verify this. It turns out none of the websites are actually using just this three word keyword phrase by itself. It seems to always be used as part of another phrase. Could we rank for it based on that? Possibly, but we would be better served trying to rank for longer versions of the phrase. I actually tested this theory and built an article based upon just the three words to see how it would do. It actually ended up on page two after a couple weeks because other sites weren't really using this particular keyword phrase. Even so, my point is, what you really ought to be looking at are keyword phrases that are four and five or more keywords in each phrase. We're looking for phrases that are picking up traffic with low competition, but with enough searches to make it worthwhile. You also want to choose keyword phrases that will bring people to your site who may be interested in what you have to offer. It is best to target your audience and select keyword phrases that will have your site displayed when someone is trying to find you.

When you see a huge number of searches, it basically means that your keyword phrase is way too broad and does not have enough words in it. We've been talking about getting free traffic as much as possible. I have not talked very much about paid advertising strategies. That is another subject. If you were going to pay for this keyword phrase, you would get a credible number of hits on your website, but most people would get there and not know why they were there and you are paying for all of that. The reason is that with so many other phrases that include these three words, there must be many of these phrases that are unrelated to your product or service. So, that is not a good keyword phrase.

What else should you use? Let's see, here's one. It says medium competition. The phrase is "vegetarian weight-loss plan". It says it only has about 9,900 searches and 4,400 local. That is pretty good traffic and it does not have as much competition. The only problem is that the weight-loss plan I am writing about is not vegetarian. I could write an article comparing my weight-loss plan to a vegetarian weight-loss plan and pick up some of this traffic, but likely the people looking would not be interested. My experience with vegetarians is that they are not interested in anything else that might include any meat by-products whatsoever. You might notice that finding low competition keyword phrases requires five, or six, or more words. We're not going to find it in four word searches that often. If you did have a vegetarian weight-loss plan, this might be a good one to use. At 9,900, it is a reasonable amount of searches. If you were to do some investigation on this particular keyword phrase, you might find that the rest of the websites do not do that good of a job with this particular keyword phrase. Sometimes 9,900 is better than 368,000, because you have a much better chance of commanding and owning that keyword phrase on your article than you would otherwise.

Now, let's look around a little bit further. If you scroll down to view other sites being returned in our search, you will see six-week weight-loss plan. That is very specific. There are 880 searches. Should you write an article about that? It has high competition. Six-week weight-loss plan is probably some product called "The Six-week Weight-loss Plan" and people are actually searching to find its website. They know the six-week weight-loss plan, but they cannot seem to locate the site, so they go out to Google and search it. That is probably a majority of the searches. Well, whatever product that is, it is apparently doing pretty well, but it is very, very specific. You could do some research, compare your product to this one, and write an article about it. Use six-week weight-loss plan as your keyword phrase. That would only be worth it if you think you could persuade enough people already on that diet to change to yours. There is going to be a lot of people that will be looking only for the six week weight-loss plan website and already made a purchase. You certainly have a very good chance of ranking fairly high on it because it is such a unique phrase. You might be the other alternative to the six-week weight-loss plan. You might have the seven-week weight-loss plan, and yours happens to be a little bit better, and so you might pick up some of those customers. The possible prospects are already targeted traffic. People try many diets and we all wish all these people were successful losing weight, but the opportunity is for people that might be ready to try another new diet.

On the outset, though, nobody would type "six-week weight-loss plan" if they are just looking for a weight-loss plan. They are looking for a particular product, aren't they? I just wanted to throw that out there so that you know how to read these things. If you see too many searches, the top of the funnel is too wide. You have to close the opening a bit more and tighten your search phrases by using longer phrases. If you see very few searches, the top of the funnel may be way too tight. I brought up the paid search example because we are trying to rank for the free traffic, not the paid. We can throw out our net a little bit wider because we aren't paying for traffic. If you're paying for every click that hits your site, you want to squeeze the net so tight that only people that are interested in your product hit your site, but you can afford to widen the net when there are no fees.

WRITING THE ARTICLE, MY SECRET SAUCE FOR ATTRACTING TRAFFIC

You want to choose between twelve and fifteen keyword phrases while you are doing research. They should all be related. This twelve to fifteen will be your keyword phrase block. You have decided on which phrase to start with and now you are going to create a post in your blog. Make sure the proper SEO work is done. **Doc Stone Tip:** Do not write the article first. That is backwards. Choose the keyword phrase first, and then write the article. If you get nothing else from me, remember this rule. Do the research, find the keyword phrase that is going to get you enough traffic with as little competition as possible, and then write the article based upon the keyword phrase. If you do it this way, you will get traffic out of it. If you do it backwards, you will have to reword your article and that gets you in all kinds of trouble. If you've always been writing the article first, and then trying to do the SEO work, or not doing the SEO work at all, then your SEO has most likely been ineffective to this point.

There are three Meta tags that are foundational for every article and page. I call it the TDK. It stands for Title, Description, and Keywords. Blogs also have what is called TAGs.

Doc Stone Tip: Note: *You should have an SEO Plugin of some kind installed and activated on your blog for this to work like I am describing. I use the All-In-One SEO Plugin.*

There are two search engines we are trying to rank for, not just one. The two search engines are Google's blog search and Google's regular search. You are familiar with Google's regular search engine; most of us use it every day. We want to be able to get into both. The page SEO - Title, Description, and Keywords - is only available if you install a SEO plugin of some kind. There is one called All in One SEO plugin. That is the one I've been using. It works very well and it ought to be built-in to WordPress, but it is not. Most of your competition writing blogs do not have a plugin like this. It has only been available for a few years so this gives you a tremendous opportunity to beat up your competition. Tags are part of WordPress. They are analogous to keyword phrases only for blogs. I teach you to use both.

THE DIFFERENCE BETWEEN BLOG SEARCH AND GOOGLE'S REGULAR SEARCH

This is a side note. It is something I have to mention. Throughout this book I have suggested using the keyword phrases for each article for both the TDK Keyword area of the SEO plugin and also using those same phrases, unchanged, for the Tags which are the phrases to be used for Google's Blog Search engine. For those of you more advanced, I have noticed this through use. Google's regular search is hardly usable for less than four words in a phrase. It seems impossible to find anything. This is not true in Google's blog search. There is no tool I'm aware of to do any kind of meaningful keyword phrase research for Google's blog search. I've noticed through writing code to display blog search information, that many times more than four words will not return any information. You may want to edit the phrases you have used for the SEO plugin and make the phrases shorter or four words or less for the tags. For those of you that need a way to research this yourself - you will have to contact me directly through Skype or from my website http://www.Internetsalesfunnel.com for more information. There is a way.

BACK TO OUR ARTICLE

You have your keyword phrase. Now you want to write that first article. The keyword phrase is going to be the title. You will use this phrase as both the title at the top of the post and the title in your SEO plugin. You are going to use the keyword phrase at least twice in your article. As you are writing your article, you are going to determine how to creatively use your keyword phrase in such a fashion that it looks and sounds coherent. Bold one of the keyword phrases. Create a link to another article that is related to the phrase on your blog if possible, but the other article must be related. If you've done the research for your keyword phrase, you will have a rough idea what your competition is doing with their SEO because you are looking for this same information on their page. Remember, you want to do just one step better. You do not want to make it look like you are trying to pack your page with keyword phrases.

You need to add your WordPress tags. WordPress tags are the blog keyword phrases. Remember to edit the number of keyword phrases to less than four each for tags only. You have your block of twelve to fifteen phrases. One of them will be the keyword phrase we've chosen for this article – the one you used in the title, description, and twice in the body. Make that the first one in the list. Add the rest until you've added all twelve to fifteen. Contrary to popular belief, even though you can put twelve to fifteen keyword phrases on your page, you can really only optimize a page for one keyword phrase. That is why we do a block of articles. Variations of keyword phrases help you strengthen your position like we saw with "weight-loss plans". There were free weight-loss plans, healthy weight-loss plans, and all of those different variations. We are also going to have to complete the SEO elements that the plugin asks for. That would be the description and keywords. Separate each one with a space and a comma. These are going to be the keywords for the page SEO. Make the description an excerpt of the article, but try and creatively use the keyword phrase in the description. Again, all you need to do is just one keyword phrase better than your competition. If you do not need to use it in the description to be one better, do not use it.

When you are done with the first article, complete your block of articles using all twelve to fifteen keyword phrases. Each article should be a completely different, original, unique article. Update the SEO elements in the same way making the title keyword phrase the first each time in the SEO plugin keyword field and the tag field.

It is not that complicated, is it? It sounds almost too easy, but that is what it is all about and that is my big secret. Essentially, what you've done is use the keyword phrase enough times on a page to outdo your competition by one and you've used twelve to fifteen related phrases strengthening your all around position in that group of related phrases. It is a legitimate, white hat set of articles written about a particular subject with all of the SEO work done to it, both for WordPress blog search and for Google's regular search. That is it. That is all this takes.

If you do it in this manner; find the keyword phrase *first,* and then write the article - you will start picking up traffic on every single one of these pages. Over the course of a year, you are going to command a large amount of traffic - free traffic, targeted traffic - coming to your website. This is what it is all about. There are a lot of other things you can do to bring in traffic which we've talked about, but this is critical work. If you do not do the SEO TDK (Title, Description, and Keywords) and the WordPress tags and you just write the title and the body, it is not worth writing from a sales standpoint. Nobody will find it. Why bother?

As an example, I wrote a little article and I used the keyword phrase "weight-loss plan". I took my advice and bolded the keyword phrase in the body of the article. I then made a link to "Get more information on a great Weight Loss Plan here". It takes readers to an affiliate page where they could sign up or buy the product. I used the phrase in the title. Again, it is not the best keyword phrase, but I was experimenting. Then I scrolled down to the categories area in my WordPress editor and I picked an existing category and I created a new category called weight-loss plan. I added the article to these categories. I have a list of twelve to fifteen keyword phrases. It always includes my name and the name of the product and some variations all on weight-loss plans of some kind. I put them in the tags area and I added them to the page SEO provided by the plugin. There are a lot of ways I could improve this article. For example, I should add a web form for an autoresponder. If I had a banner or a graphic I could use within the article that flashed, or if I added a short video for the people that do not or won't read. If I had something that came from the manufacturer like a white paper that I could give away in return for signing up to my newsletter, even better. If it is a YouTube video, right click on any YouTube video and you will get the HTML embed code from it. Paste it in the text side of the editor. There are a lot of ways to improve the effectiveness of this article. What I'm showing you is how to get people to view your article in the first place. The article needs traffic and visitors to be read.

Another part of our marketing is analytics. It is wonderful to have a page or article out performing for us, but just exactly how effective is it? How are you going to know if it is doing well? You can use Google Analytics. Click on http://www.analytics.google.com or http://www.google.com/analytics. If you have a Gmail account, then once you've logged into Gmail, you will be able to go right into these sites without signing up. **Doc Stone Tip:** *You need a Gmail account for many things, get one.* Track your particular article or page if you want to see if what I'm telling you works or not. When you are all done and have entered all the information that Google asks for, you will end up with a tracking code. It is just some HTML. Highlight it, copy it, and go out to your post. Put it in text mode, which is HTML mode, and up at the top in the body, paste it and save it. The code you add is invisible and does not show, but now you are tracking all traffic on the page or article you want analytics from.

I tested another article called "Does Webfire Work?" Webfire is an incredible set of SEO tools that makes finding keywords that work a whole lot easier. Somebody actually went out and bought doeswebfirework.com. That took first spot of course. But using the methods I just described, my article ranked third on the page within a week.

I want you to know that I have done extensive testing over the years and everything you read in this book is what I know and believe to be true. Maybe it sounds like I only did a few tests here and there and made some conclusions based on just these examples, but nothing could be farther from the truth. I started working with the internet well before there were search engines. I've worked with just about every advertising method available over the years either on the internet, through the mail, or printed. The examples you are reading about are just the ones I've chosen to illustrate in more detail for you.

Here's one of those things that people do. If you are really doing well with a particular keyword phrase, and the phrase itself is available as a dot com website, buy it and start using it. It can bump you towards the top as long as your article or product topic matches.

The point of all of this is; if you use my methods and build a page a week, you will enjoy a significant amount of free targeted traffic to your website. The more your site grows and the higher the ranking, the sooner you will achieve *Web Authority*. The site that Google feels is the authority for a particular topic gets the lion's share of all available traffic within reasonable distance of the keyword phrases used. Whatever your niche, if you follow these methods, you will soon achieve the results you want. If you are in a unique niche, that will happen very quickly. If you are in a very competitive niche, it will take longer. That will depend on writing ability and SEO prowess of your competitors.

Do not forget, articles written less than once a week and Google's blog search may forget you exist. Google's regular search engine has more longevity. That is why we use both. I'm not talking about much work, one article a week on your topic. You can do it.

We discussed needing product pages, at least two for each product you sell. Product articles have a payment button and are directly related to creating our revenue. We discussed needing informational pages which are about your topic and lots of them over time. Informational articles bring targeted search traffic to your site. We discussed needing viral articles that are to be published on an article marketing directory website. Viral articles bring you links that help us rank higher with search engines. An article that gets thirty to fifty links is a great article. It might take you a couple of months to get that many links. If only ten percent of all the traffic available for each keyword phrase became yours, you would be realizing at least a couple of hundred hits per month from each article. If you keep writing these articles for an entire year, fifty two articles each receiving 250 to 500 hits per month would generate 13000 to 26000 hits per month. All of these visitors are targeted prospects. That means the person doing the search is looking for somebody like you, and typed in that keyword phrase you used. They were actually looking for what it is you are offering. They find you. If you have what they want and your product solves their problem, they will buy. That is huge. All of this traffic is free other than the time it takes to write and post the articles. That is even bigger. If you continue for a few years, you will have built yourself quite a business.

Just one more thing to remember, what I have been teaching is only one traffic method, but it is the most important one. When times get tight, these methods will continue to work for you and it does not cost any money. You will always get a little extra traffic on each one of them.

THE LAST WORD

I want to challenge you. Become part of our team, share your ideas, share your products, but please share your blogs with us. Come find me on skype, contact name 'salesnav', and join our community. Please join the newsletter at the site below and come to a live webinar. If you are trying to figure out how to monetize a topic you love and just can't figure out how you're going to make much money at it, give me a shot at it. For me, it's a challenge and one I really enjoy. I hope you'll visit soon.

There is a lot more to Internet marketing and this book only covers section 18 of my huge library of online webinars. I urge you to visit http://www.Internetsalesfunnel.com for more on setting up the rest of your funnel and more on traffic generation.

Table of Contents

RESOURCES

AD ROTATOR PPC ORGANIC LEAD SITES

Advertise Your Business Now

Prospect Geyser

Lead Gusher

InternetTVTraffic

Swat Prospector

TRAINING SITES

Contact List Builder

Video Genesis

Marketing Genesis

Traffic Genesis

Evergreen Business Systems

Webinar Jam

SOCIAL NETWORKING

Sweeva

SoKule

Traffic Swarm

TOOLS

OneTimeOfferTemplates

Banner Creator

Banner Maker

Evergreen Business Systems

Kajabi

Deal Guardian

Click Bank

Payoneer

Webfire

Paypal

DOMAIN NAME REGISTRARS

http://www.godaddy.com

http://www.namecheap.com

http://www.networksolutions.com

https://www.domainnames.com

https://www.onlydomains.com

DOMAIN NAME REGISTRATION INFORMATION SERVICES

http://www.whois.com

http://www.alexa.com

HOSTING COMPANY I SUGGEST - *Hosting, Autoresponder, Squeeze Page Templates, Conference Room and Video Hosting all in one for 9.97/month*

http://www.hostthenprofit.com

EXITSPLASH

Exit Splash

SQUEEZE PAGES

AdKreator

Instant Squeezepage Generator

Instant Splash

Point and Click Squeeze

Splash Page Maker

USEFUL SITES AND TOOLS

Free Favicon Free Favicon Generator

Hits Connect Ad tracker system

Axandra Website Submission Software

Logo Creator Create Logos

Skype Instant Messaging

Voice Over Talent

Royalty Free Business Music

HTML EDITORS

Dreamweaver HTML Editor Not Free, but this is the cadillac and what Doc uses

Coffee Cup HTML Editor Free simple HTML editors here and below, require FTP

SeaMonkey Project

Kompozer HTML Editor

ACCOUNTING, PRO-FORMA, AND BUDGETING

Quickbooks Full G/L Accounting Software

Quicken CheckBook Software

Peachtree Accounting by Sage

Personal Finance Software with Budgeting

Google Expense Tracking Templates Online

This covers just about every kind of expense tracking you'd ever need

U.S. Home Office Deductions Guidelines

Microsoft Home Budget Templates

Microsoft Home Business Templates

188

Business Planning and Pro-Forma PDFs and Spreadsheets

Look for Pro Form Microsoft Templates

Pro Forma Help and Finding a Loan

Small Business Administration (SBA) Loans

FTP FILE TRANSFER SOFTWARE

Filezilla

SmartFTP

Coffee CUP FTP

Panic

Cute FTP

GRAPHICS

DaFont - Create your own font for your signature – download, right-click choose install

Adobe After Effects - Adobe Animation Software

After Effects Templates

ZIP PROGRAMS

7-Zip

WinZip

WinRAR

JZip

ANALYTICS

Google Analytics

Sitemeter

Crazy EggGoogle Analytics

GOOGLE WEBMASTER TOOLS

Google Places

Google Site Verification and Web Master Tools

Google Keyword Toolbox

ESSENTIAL WORDPRESS PLUGINS

Akismet - To alleviate spam, totally free

Coffee 2 Code - Preserve Source Code formatting (Very specialized if you want to display html code for example, you need this)

Blogging in Microsoft Word

SEO TOOLS AND KEYWORD TOOLS

Webfire - Professional Search Engine SEO Tools

Google Adwords Google PPC Pay Per Click Ads

BingAds Bing/Yahoo/Microsoft PPC Pay Per Click Ads

Keyword Spy Keyword Research

SemRush See your competitors' organic positions

Keyword Eye Keywords. Visualized. Simplified

SCRIPTS

http://www.butterflyopensourcecode.com/devnetwork

OUTSOURCING

oDesk, the On Demand Global Workforce ODesk enables its users to hire, manage, and pay technology service providers around the world. http://www.odesk.com/

Outsourcing to Freelance Programmers, Web & Logo Designers, Writers, Illustrators on Elance Global marketplace matching buyers and sellers of services that can be easily delivered over the Web, by fax, phone, email or mail. http://www.elance.com/

Custom Web Design and Programming. Freelance Programmers. Outsource Web Development Outsourcing Offering temporary placement for programming, web design, and copywriting. http://getafreelancer.com/

GetACoder - Quick & Easy Project Outsourcing. Outsource Your Project Today. Custom Programming and Web Design. Freelance programmers and web designers. ... Thousands of outsourced jobs prove that GetACoder is a cost-effective way to get ... http://www.getacoder.com/

Guru.com - The world's largest online marketplace for freelance talent. Resource for freelancers and consultants, with career advice, job listings, columns, tips, and other information. http://www.guru.com/

ScriptLance.com Custom Freelance Programming. Outsource web projects to programmers and designers. Freelance web

designers and software programmers. http://www.scriptlance.com/

Rent A Coder: How Software Gets Done -- Home of the worlds' largest ... Rent a coder is an international marketplace where people who need custom ... "After a visit to RentACoder.com...I got. something I needed for a ... http://www.rentacoder.com/

Freelance Web Designers, Programmers, Writers. Custom Web Design. Freelance Projects & Jobs Freelance work marketplace where clients can post programming, design, writing, SEO, or other type of job requests and receive bids from freelance professionals. http://www.project4hire.com/

WEBINAR AND CONFERENCE SOFTWARE

GVO-Conference

GVO HostThenProfit Autoresponder, Squeeze Page Templates, Site Hosting, Video Hosting and Recorder, and Conference Room

WebinarJam

ARTICLE MARKETING SITES

http://www.goarticles.com

http://www.articlesnatch.com

http://www.articledashboard.com

http://www.articlealley.com.

http://www.hubpages.com

http://www.sooperarticles.com

http://www.articlebase.com

http://www.selfgrowth.com.

www.ingramcontent.com/pod-product-compliance
Lightning Source LLC
Chambersburg PA
CBHW060554200326
41521CB00007B/568